Life-Confidence For Kids!

How to Programme Your Child for Success and Help Them Discover Their True Potential

Sue Atkinson

Publisher Data & Legal Information
Published by Harecroft Publishing
ISBN 978-0-9571138-0-0
First edition, November 2011.
Copyright © 2011, Sue Atkinson. All rights reserved.
Contact the Author at sue@lifeconfidenceforkids.com
Website: www.lifeconfidenceforkids.com

Every attempt has been made by the author to provide acknowl-
edgement of the sources used for the material in this book. If there
has been an omission please contact the author at the address
above.

To Jane and Neil
I love you

Contents

Reading and Listening 225

Acknowledgements

My heartfelt thanks goes to all those who have helped towards making this book a reality: To all the friends who lent their support and kindly took the time to read drafts giving me many useful comments. To my mentor Frank Garon for 'cracking the whip' and keeping me on track until the book was completed. To Rhonda and Paul at Awaken the Author Within for their knowledgeable help and guidance. To Janardhan Saithala for technical help; to my son-in-law Brian (who has the patience of Job) for giving so freely of his time to help me to get my head around the technicalities (no mean feat!) and for being instrumental in getting the book published. To my son Neil for so willingly burning the midnight oil to help with the formatting. To my daughter Jane for proof-reading the final copy and helping and advising me in so many other ways. To my husband John for always being there for me and being such a strong support throughout all the ups and the downs, and the blood, sweat and tears! And last but not least, to all those precious children who, throughout the years, have taught me so much – especially my own children – I feel privileged to have you in my life.

Preamble

How much thought do you give to the things you say to your children?

When it comes to life success, the overriding quality which affects what we achieve in life above all others is confidence. In every situation, from job interviews and career advancement to relationships both in business and social life, to success with a sport or a personal skill, confidence is indisputably one of the most important qualities you can possess.

Young minds are like an empty book just waiting to be written; a brand new PC just waiting to be programmed! What are you programming your child's mind with? As parents we all want what's best for our children and we all do the best job we can do given the experience we have – but is that good enough?

Helping your child to grow up into a confident, self-assured young adult could be the most satisfying and fulfilling journey you will ever make. It's undoubtedly a journey which will influence your child's future happiness for the rest of their lives.

Congratulations! You have just taken an important step towards giving your child one of the best gifts you can give – **Supreme Life-Confidence!**

First Things First

About Me

For those of you who don't know me let me introduce myself. My name's Sue Atkinson and I live in Surrey UK, with my dogs, horse, and menagerie of other animals and my long-suffering husband John!

My two children, Jane and Neil, were 'pushed from the nest' some 10 years ago (actually they flew willingly!) They say they are grateful for all the things I did right and, I am happy to say, have forgiven me for all the things I did wrong! And we now have a wonderful close, best-friend relationship, for which I am ever grateful.

I have been a teacher for 40 years now, having had a variety of roles including head of infants and acting deputy head, and I have taught a wide age range from reception (age 4) through to 6th form college students.

I took time out from my teaching career to enjoy bringing up my own children (making all the mistakes I'm about to tell you not to make!) and during that time I ran my own children's book business, giving talks to parents, play groups and schools.

I qualified with distinction as a Life Coach with The Coaching Academy and am a Chartered Facilitator of personal development seminars for LifeSuccess Productions. I also offer Confidence Workshops for schools.

So what drives me to write about such an important subject?

Simple: I was a child with no confidence!

I grew up with a self-esteem that was lower than a snake's belly – and you can't get lower than that! It has taken me many years and much perseverance to get the level of confidence I have now and my mission is to let my journey be of benefit to others.

I certainly don't pretend to have all the answers (my journey is an ongoing one) and you are free to disagree with some of the things I say – which is as it should be. I do however speak as someone who has had first hand experience of working with children in the areas covered in this book and I have made many mistakes to learn from along the way.

If you would like to find out more about Life-Confidence Coaching for you or your child go to:

www.lifeconfidenceforkids.com

or you can contact me at

sue@lifeconfidenceforkids.com

I'd be delighted to hear from you.

About This Book

Protection of Privacy

Throughout the book I have included anecdotes of real life situations to illustrate my points. Whilst the stories are all true, to protect privacy the names I have used are fictitious.

On a Technical Note

Firstly, in order to avoid discrimination I have interspersed both the masculine and feminine gender throughout the book.

Secondly, whilst many of the examples relate to younger children, The B.E.S.T. Success Formula is generic therefore equally applicable to children of all ages. In fact, applying the concepts from this formula is an absolute necessity for anyone wanting to achieve a happier, more successful, fulfilled life – and it's never too late to start.

Thirdly, please interpret the term 'parents' to imply the child's chief carers. That said, *"Life-Confidence For Kids!"* is not only for parents, carers and parents-to-be. I hope it will also be a valuable reference for teachers, social workers, youth workers, aunts, uncles, grand parents – in fact anyone who is involved with young people, from toddlers to teens, and has the best interest of those young people at heart.

How to Use This Book

There are certain parts of this book which I suggest you read first and other parts which can be dipped into. Generally speaking you should read through the book up to Chapter 7. There are some very powerful concepts to grasp – particularly in Chapters 4 – 7. I have tried not to make them too technical. Please don't skip them – I have put them at the beginning because they are crucial to your understanding of the importance of the rest of the book. From chapter 8 onwards you can either continue to read through the chapters in order, or dip into them as the mood takes you.

You and Your Child

When I first started writing this book I attempted to keep the development of your children as an isolated section, separate from your own personal journey of self-growth and your self-confidence as a parent – I failed – miserably! If there is one thing that has come out of this exercise it's this:

 Your own self-improvement, both as an individual and as a parent or carer, is inextricably intertwined with the ongoing development of your children.

So whilst I have tried to keep some sort of structure for easier reading, I make no excuse for frequently moving back and forth between:

    1. You as a person.

    2. You as a parent/carer.

    3. Your child.

Every tip and strategy related to your children can, and should, also be applied to yourself and vice versa. Expecting your child to be confident if you are lacking confidence yourself would be like expecting them to eat vegetables whilst watching you eat cream cakes and chocolate!

The purpose of this book then, is to show you ways you can help your children to build their confidence and bring out the genius which undoubtedly lies within them, whilst developing your own confidence at the same time.

The bonus is the resulting understanding you will gain, which I hope will launch you on the journey of freeing some of your own limiting beliefs – beliefs which are holding you back from being the very best you can be.

Your Child's Self-Image

When children are very young they are totally uninhibited and this is a big part of their charm. Sadly this doesn't last long. As they grow up they are fed a myriad of subliminal messages from the outside world, which influences the way they see themselves (their self-image).

When these messages are heavily balanced on the negative side, as they so often are, they create inhibitions and your child's true self gets buried deeper and deeper within. However confident you think your child may be, you can bet your life there will be situations when their self-esteem will dip and their self-image will need a boost.

Children form an image of themselves by the time they are 5 years old and they gradually become more and more inhibited as they pick up on criticism from the world around them. As an adult it takes a lot more work to change the way we think about ourselves, so whatever the age of your children, the sooner you begin to help them build a more positive self-image, the better.

As they grow older, their inbuilt need for the good opinion of others makes them hide their true, natural self for fear of not being accepted.

What makes this so tragic is this paradox:

 When we have the confidence to relax and act naturally – in anyone's company – and be independent of what other people might think of us, we are far more likely to gain their good opinion!

It is only then, when we are being our true authentic self, that our full potential can be unleashed and it is this state of 'inner being' which forms a major part of the self-fulfilment puzzle for our children as they grow into adulthood.

Your job as a parent/carer then, is to help your child to build a resistance to the negative conditioning and influences from the outside world and to gain the confidence needed to help him not just to cope, but to truly shine. Only then will he become a well balanced individual, who is unafraid of being himself.

And *that's* what *"Life-Confidence For Kids!"* is all about.

The Three C's

There are three main strands throughout this book and your ability to help your children to develop unshakable life-confidence will depend directly upon how well you develop your skills in these three areas.

I call them The 3 **C**'s – they are:

Consciousness, **C**ommunication and **C**ollaboration.

Let's put in the fourth **C** for fun:

CONSCIOUSNESS + COMMUNICATION + COLLABORATION

= CONFIDENT KIDS!

CONSCIOUSNESS

Consciousness in this context is all about developing your own awareness as a person in order to become an effective parent.

We will be looking at the importance of developing and maintaining your consciousness or your awareness of how you have been conditioned to think, and the limiting beliefs you have grown up with, which you are inadvertently passing on to your children. You may get a few surprises here!

COMMUNICATION

Both the verbal and non-verbal messages you communicate to your children are instrumental in shaping their future lives. Learning how to communicate positive messages through the way you act, the way you interact, and the things you say, is of paramount importance. This cannot be overstated.

What's more, when you begin to take on board some of the concepts in this book, you will be well on the way to becoming an excellent role model for your children to follow.

COLLABORATION

Collaboration here simply means the way you work together with your child as a 'team'. It is all about the partnership and mutual respect which you develop with your children, resulting in their growing sense of ownership and responsibility for their own actions. It's about a way of interacting with them to help them become self-reliant and realise that they have the power to solve their own problems and to see themselves as an important part of the solution. Confidence comes not only from feeling secure and loved unconditionally, but from feeling valued and from having your contributions and ideas listened to and respected.

"Life-Confidence For Kids!" will equip you with lots of practical ideas, tools and methods which you can use with your children to help them take responsibility and build their confidence.

How This Book is Set Out

This book is set out in 6 parts as follows:

PART 1 The BEST Gift

In Part 1 I first of all establish a clear definition of what I mean by life-confidence.

I then examine the role of schools and just how much they contribute towards developing this important skill.

Next I introduce The B.E.S.T. Success Formula which embraces what I call The Four Pillars of Life-Confidence. These are the four crucial factors which are the indispensable ingredients of life-success and fulfilment. Each is a vital part of the confidence puzzle.

When you help your child to develop all four of these life-skills on a continuous daily basis you will, without question, equip her with the confidence to achieve her full potential and grow up to live a truly happy and fulfilled life.

In the following Parts 2, 3, 4 and 5 I cover the components of The B.E.S.T. Success Formula in detail and give you the tools and the strategies to implement its development in both your own life and that of your child.

PART 2 The First Pillar: Belief

Part 2 is dedicated to helping you to build your child's self-belief through building both your own belief in yourself as a parent and your belief in the potential of your child. I talk about the importance of the part you play and give you the concepts and the many proven strategies for you to use in your everyday interaction with your child.

Here I explain in simple terms how our minds, and the minds of our children, actually work. To get the most benefit from this book, it is crucial that you fully understand this concept. You are advised to read and re-read it until you have absorbed it sufficiently to grasp the importance of its message.

It illustrates the enormous potential each and every child is born with and explains the process we, as parents, need to go through to get into the habit of thinking positive, having positive belief in our children and creating the positive environment needed for them to thrive and flourish.

This section also explains the pitfalls to watch out for and the way to go about creating that positive environment. It deals with the negative language you are most probably using when talking to your children, without even realising it, and talks about the ways in which you can boost their confidence simply by changing the words you use.

PART 3 The Second Pillar: Enthusiasm

No matter how badly you want your children to succeed, at the end of the day it's over to them. Enthusiasm is a necessary component of anything worth achieving in life – and no less so with children – but motivating your child is not always easy.

In this part I talk about how you can help children to set goals which will inspire them into action without you having to 'crack the whip'. Keeping up that enthusiasm when there are obstacles in the way can sometimes be a challenge, so you will learn ways to teach your children how to keep focused and on task.

PART 4 The Third Pillar: Self-Love

In this section you will learn ways to build your child's self-worth, self-esteem and self-image – all necessary ingredients of life-confidence. I explore what is meant by Emotional Intelligence: how we can help children to manage their feelings and have a positive impact on the feelings of others; how to deal with conflicts and build a harmonious relationship with your child; and how to help them to form harmonious relationships with their peers and develop strong social and emotional competences.

PART 5 The Fourth Pillar: Targeted Action Steps

In Part 5 you will not only learn more about how to set goals, but also how to achieve them. This is the action part. Here I show you how to help your children to build success upon success.

You will learn how to work with them to break their goals down into baby steps which I call TARGETED ACTION STEPS, and these will form the stepping stones to their success.

PART 6 The Way Forward

The final section offers a summary and suggested actions to set you on your way to implementing what you have learnt.

Certainly no one thing works with all of the children all of the time, and the receptivity to these ideas will depend on the child, the time, the place and the mood of the moment.

The concepts in this book however have been tried and tested by countless experts in the field of personal growth, and the fact that, at the time of writing, Emotional Intelligence is gradually filtering through to teachers via inset training days is testimony to the growing belief in its importance.

Whoever you are, I salute you for seeking to grow yourself and to help the children in your care to grow. The very fact that you are reading this book means you are open to improvement and are aware that, however experienced we may be, we always have something to learn.

There are many powerful strategies contained in these pages, and if you learn just one thing from reading this book which you didn't know before, that one thing could turn out to be of priceless value in shaping the future of a young life. As a result, my efforts will have all been worthwhile.

So now let's have a look at the importance of your role:

About You

Actions Speak Louder Than Words
Confident Children Need Confident Parents
A Virtuous Circle
Keeping An Open Mind
Getting the Balance Right
A Moment to Reflect

As you learn more about the strategies I am going to talk about in the context of child-development, as mentioned earlier you are going to need to do a bit of work on yourself.

You may still be asking, *"Why does a book about building confidence in children need to have an entire section dedicated to talking about me?"*

Good question! It leads me to two important facts which explain why, as a parent, you are the most important person in this whole equation.

Fact 1 *The first five years is an intense learning and developmental period in a child's life. Brain growth is massive during this time*[1]

Fact 2 *Parents or primary carers, are a child's first role model. They are at once both the first and the most powerful role model whom their children look up to in their early years.*

Combine these two facts with the fact that kids are copiers, and it is clear to see how crucial your role really is. Every little thing you say and do in those early years, is soaked up by your children like a sponge!

---

[1] http://extension.umaine.edu/publications/4356e/ Children and Brain Development: What We Know About How Children Learn. For further research on brain development: http://nccic.acf.hhs.gov/poptopics/brain.html

Actions Speak Louder Than Words

Not only are kids copiers, they are very perceptive. I have already emphasised the importance of being aware of the words we use when we speak to our children and I shall be talking about that in detail later. However, even more important is the way we convey our words i.e. our body language and tone of voice.

If you want your children to embrace the concepts in this book you need to embrace them yourself. If *you* don't believe what you are saying your children won't believe it either.

Confident Children Need Confident Parents

To help them become confident you must also be confident yourself. The two go hand in hand. You are the person they look up to. You are the person they will emulate. You need to **be** the person you want them to be.

Whether you are new to the field of personal growth or you have 'the cap, the badge and the T shirt' – no matter – you will still need to do regular developmental checks on yourself alongside working with your children. It's not enough just to read a self-help book then put it aside and carry on with your life as before. Developing your self-growth doesn't happen overnight. It's a wonderful, never ending journey of self-discovery and fulfilment.

Once you take that first step; once you glimpse that inviting golden road strewn with a mixture of flowers and weeds along the way; once you taste the bitter sweet mixture of tears and treasures, frustration and fulfilment – you are hooked.... and the rewards are priceless.

Like any skill, personal growth takes practice and must be applied on a regular daily basis. It's an awareness which needs to be constantly worked at until it becomes an inseparable part of you.

When you embark on the road of personal-development you will very likely begin to feel you can't get enough of self-help reading.

You're right. You can't get enough. The day you say, "I've learnt enough, I don't need any more", is the day you stop growing.

Self-development is like a reference book of life which you take with you wherever you go, repeatedly referring to its pages until they are folded down, written on, cross-referenced, dog-eared, worn, torn, faded and creased and gradually become indelibly etched onto your mind.

If repetition is the first law of learning ... even more powerful is reading the same message, from different sources, expressed in different ways, as this makes it far more likely you'll take it in.

If you want self-confidence to become a habit, it needs to be constantly worked at until it becomes a natural way to be.

However, it must be said...

 All the thinking and reading in the world will not bring about change unless it is followed by ACTION!

– i.e. applying the principles in your own life on a regular daily basis.

This book contains some simple but very powerful actions you can take to bring about profound changes, both in your own life and that of your children, whatever their age.

Since the days of the ancient Greek philosophers man has been searching for 'the way' to achieve a life of fulfilment and happiness and there have been many great authors on the subject.

Since first embarking on my own journey of self-growth, over the years I have amassed a large collection of personal-development books and CD/DVD programmes. I have attended numerous motivational seminars, listened to countless talks on the subject and studied many courses, and have come to the conclusion that every one is saying the same thing in a variety of different ways, namely:

 To change the results we are getting in our lives we must first change the way we think.

And so it follows that:

 To change the results our children are getting in their *lives we must help them to change the way* they *think*.

A Virtuous Circle

In his programme *'Creating Miracles Every Day'*, Richard Carlson refers to 'a virtuous circle'. Unlike a vicious circle, which we strive to get out of, a virtuous circle is something great to be in.

The wonderful thing about learning how to help others, especially our own children, is the virtuous circle it creates – the knock-on effect it has on ourselves. When you help your children to grow you cannot help but grow yourself, and the more you grow yourself, the more you can help your children.

You will very likely find yourself taking the concepts from this book and embracing them within other areas of your life too.

In addition to developing your own self-awareness, you will improve the quality of all your relationships, as well as those with your children, because you will have a greater understanding of what makes people 'tick'.

So I'm going to ask you to make a commitment: When it comes to working with your children – instead of just paying lip service to an idea (which children quickly see through), plunge into it. Dive, splash and wallow alongside them until you learn to 'swim' together. Adapt all the ideas and embrace them fully into your own self-growth.

Keeping An Open Mind

"Life-Confidence For Kids!" has been written to give you suggestions to try out and targets to aim for and to help you to develop a positive mindset when it comes to the job of bringing up children.

There will be times when certain strategies don't work for you, but don't give up; if you practise applying them consistently, there will be still other times when they work like a dream.

Do keep an open mind. If something doesn't gel with you please don't dismiss it out of hand – if you do, you will be doing yourself and your children a grave disservice – just put it on the 'back burner' to revisit again when it feels right.

As parents we never get it right all of the time and it is important to remember that you are human and you will make mistakes, and not to beat yourself up when you do. Always look for what you can learn from your mistakes and you will always find something.

Use your intuition. A lot of the things you do and say will be the right things to do and say at the time. No-one knows your children better than you do and that special bond you have with them will give you an instinctive understanding of how to respond in many situations.

This book is meant to give you a guideline, a standard to aspire to, and as long as you are using more positive strategies than negative ones you will be on the right road.

If you do take some of the things I tell you about on board (which I sincerely hope will be the case) I truly believe you will be giving your children a head start in this big wide world of ours, where it's all too easy to get your confidence knocked and your spirits broken.

Getting the Balance Right

Helping your children to become happy, balanced, self-confident people is a bit like helping them to ride a bike. You can't keep the balance for them, you can only hold onto the saddle until, with constant repetition, encouragement and belief that they can do it, they finally become sufficiently proficient for you to let go.

We can use this metaphor with the many other things which children learn as they grow up, like learning to walk, talk, read, and write.

We can only teach them by demonstration, redirect them when they deviate, pick them up when they fall, dust them off, get them back on track and push them on their way again – whilst all the time believing in them. But in essence, they have to do the work themselves.

Developing their life-confidence is similar. We must lead by example, help them keep their balance and then be there to help them come back when they go off course, whilst constantly demonstrating an unshakeable belief in their abilities.

As you work through this book, my aim is for you to reach the stage when you are confident in the knowledge that, when you let go of that saddle, you will be sending your child into a well balanced future life, equipped with the confidence to deal with whatever life throws at her – and come out on top.

Then you will have put the foundations in place to give her the best chance of happiness and success and you will be reassured by the fact that you gave her your best shot.

A Moment to Reflect

"Writing is the doing part of thinking"

Glenn Dietzel

So before we go any further let me ask you to pause for a moment's reflection. Just think about your relationship with your child and the many situations you have to deal with daily.

Now write down three areas which you would most like to improve.

Maybe you would like her to be tidier. You may have an issue with getting her to do her homework or getting her up in the morning, or she may have friendship problems or worries about exams or tests. There could be many things which need addressing, but for now just choose two or three of the main ones which are the most important for you.

Now, by the side of each one, write down ideally how you would like things to be and we will re-visit this later.

As you work through this book it may help to make notes of specific ideas and strategies which you could apply to these three areas.

So let's get started.

Hold on tight, you're in for a great journey!

PART 1

The BEST Gift

*"The foundation quality of success in any
walk of life is self-confidence"*
Brian Tracey

Chapter 1

The Magic Ingredient of Success

The Foundation for Happiness
The Foundation for Fulfillment
The Foundation for Health and Well-Being
The Foundation for Success
Lee's Story

Over the years, throughout both my personal life and my career, I have come to the conclusion that there is one important ingredient in the recipe of life which, above all others, will greatly increase your child's success and happiness, and I have named that ingredient **'Life-Confidence'**.

Life-confidence is without doubt the overriding quality which affects everything we achieve in life. What exactly do I mean by life-confidence? What is its place in today's education system? Why should it be given equal, if not more, importance to other areas of the school curriculum... and why isn't it? I aim to answer all these questions and more. First let me begin by clarifying what I mean by life-confidence.

I have used the term 'Life-Confidence' because I believe it more accurately describes what this book is about. A person can be *self*-confident in certain areas of life and not in others. For example the same person can be *self*-confident when it comes to driving a car, but totally lacking in self-confidence when going for an interview.

Life-confidence on the other hand, is about having a general inner confidence and self-esteem; an ability to interact with other people with ease and to deal with any obstacle or circumstance which comes along. It's about being self-confident in all areas of life; it's about believing in yourself; it's about having a large measure of self-worth; it's about being your own best friend.

Let me say from the start – it's important not to confuse life-confidence with arrogance. They are two very different states of being. If someone is arrogant they have an air of superiority and are keen to give the impression that they know it all. In fact the extent of their knowledge will always be limited by virtue of the fact that they are not open to learn more.

Such people are often insecure individuals who feel the need to prove themselves by demonstrating how good they are to the rest of the world.

Life-confidence, on the other hand, is a way of being which comes from within. The life-confident person will freely admit they have a lot to learn, but at the same time have a quiet air of self-assurance. They will be decisive and will not need the approval of others before taking action. In Dr. Wayne Dyer's words, they will have *"A strong, self-image immunity to the fear of criticism and making mistakes"*, and what's more – they will recognise that mistakes are an opportunity to learn and to grow.

Life-confident people are natural leaders.

Just stop and think for a minute: Think of the last time you were with someone who was supremely life-confident. How did it feel to be in their company?

Without having the self-centred need to prove themselves, life-confident people focus their attention on others and have a natural, warm and friendly energy. They are relaxed and you feel at ease when you are with them. They are the people whom others seek out because it's so uplifting to be in their energy field. They are charismatic and attract abundance wherever they go because they are their true, authentic self.

I hope you are beginning to see that life-confidence is the very best gift you can possibly give to your children.

A strong life-confidence is the foundation for HAPPINESS, FULFIL-MENT, HEALTH and WELL-BEING and SUCCESS, all rolled into one!

Let's take a closer look at this statement for a minute:

The Foundation for Happiness

"Remember happiness doesn't depend upon who you are or what you have; it depends solely on what you think"

Dale Carnegie

Let me ask you a question:

What do you want for your children? What do you **truly** want?

Over and above the academic qualifications and the material acquisitions which our society seems obsessed by, we all, of course, want them to be happy.

But happiness, to a certain extent, is left to chance. We look upon it as something that is dependent upon outside forces and the 'cards' that life deals us; something that is elusive and outside our control, and if we attain it we consider it the result of good luck. In fact, happiness is very much within our control.

Happiness, as the song goes, means different things to different people but, suffice to say, it's about being pro-active in following your passions and realising your dreams, whatever they may happen to be.

Confident people are not afraid to go after their dreams. They are optimists. Unlike the average person they don't dwell on the reasons why something won't work – rather they prefer to think of all the reasons why it *will* work. They are not paralysed by the fear of failure. They understand that to do anything in life we must take calculated risks and they are confident enough to take those risks.

They are not prepared to stay in a job they hate, for example, for the sake of security. They are self-assured and assertive and they are willing to push out their boat in the pursuit of happiness... and because they have the confidence that they will find it – guess what? ...they usually do!

The Foundation for Fulfillment

"To find fulfilment... don't exist with life – embrace it."

Jim Beggs

Fulfilment goes hand in hand with happiness. In fact fulfilment is the prerequisite of happiness. If you are not feeling fulfilled and contented, then you can never be truly happy. Essentially fulfilment comes from within. Material achievements alone do not bring lasting fulfilment.

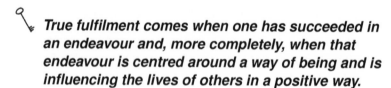 **True fulfilment comes when one has succeeded in an endeavour and, more completely, when that endeavour is centred around a way of being and is influencing the lives of others in a positive way.**

And of course, to succeed in any endeavour one must first be confident.

The Foundation for Health and Well-Being

"Health is not valued till sickness comes".

Dr. Thomas Fuller

You may be asking, "How can life-confidence have anything to do with health?" In fact it has a great deal to do with it.

We all know that excessive stress can be a killer. When faced with a challenge, lack of confidence can cause an excess of worry, fear, anxiety, sleepless nights, high blood pressure and has a knock on effect on all sorts of health related issues.

Equally dangerous to health is inertia; that inability to do anyth... g with your life because you are so lacking in confidence in your own abilities, you are afraid to take even the smallest risk. So you retreat into your comfort zone; you sink into inertia. Inertia brings boredom and depression, and when we are at a low ebb, so too is our immune system.

On Wellbeing: The dictionary definition of 'Wellbeing' is, *'Healthy, contented or prosperous condition; moral or physical welfare'*. So a lion-share of life-confidence will also undoubtedly go a long way towards achieving a state of wellbeing.

The Foundation for Success

> *"If a person advances confidently in the direction of their dreams, and endeavours to live the life they have imagined, they will meet with success unexpected in common hours"*
>
> Thoreau

Wow! How powerful is that!

I have read that quote many times and it still sends a tingle down my spine!

Life-confident people take responsibility for their successes and their failures, and if something doesn't work out they pick themselves up, dust themselves off and learn from the experience. They take charge of their lives. They never take failure personally and are always willing to try again. Their rock-solid self-belief ensures their ultimate success in whatever endeavour they choose. In fact – they couldn't avoid success if they wanted to!

At this point you may be asking, but doesn't success depend upon academic qualifications too? This of course depends on what your goals are in life. Passing exams and getting certificates are certainly a good start. However, imagine for a moment the following scenario:

Two people go for an interview for the same job. One with just a modicum of knowledge about the subject, but with a refreshing enthusiasm, a determination and willingness to learn and oodles of life-confidence; the other, very highly qualified academically but painfully shy and withdrawn and awkward in the company of others, lacking in confidence, self-conscious and unable to express themselves.

Question: – Which one do you think stands the best chance of getting the job? Which one would you employ?

Although the kind of job would be a factor to some degree – generally speaking for me the first one wins hands down.

But it's not all black and white. The interrelation between confidence and academic achievement can become a vicious circle, i.e. lack of confidence can affect exam results and poor exam results can be a blow to confidence.

There can be no doubt though that developing confidence and self-belief from an early age is the King Pin of life-success.

So what then does being 'successful' in life really mean?

Getting high qualifications and a 'good job' is career-success. A person can achieve career-success but still be unhappy. Life-success is more than that. It's about achieving a feeling of happiness and fulfilment through following our passions and living true to our values.

Let me illustrate this with the following true story:

Lee's Story

I'll always remember a boy called Lee in one of my classes at school. Academic achievement never came easy to Lee. All through his school life he struggled to keep up with the other children in his year group and he was in the lower ability group for just about everything he did.

At that time I worried about Lee's poor ability, wondering how he would fare when he had to leave school and get a job. With such poor numeracy and literacy skills how would he cope?

Eventually Lee left school, and I often wondered what had become of him.

Several years went by and one day I happened to be passing a field which was being ploughed. As the tractor passed I recognised the young man who was driving it. It was Lee! When he saw me he waved and his face lit up in a huge proud grin. He drove the tractor away across the field and as I watched I saw him turn the tractor ready to plough the next furrow.

He stopped – got out – and surveying the length of the field, he slowly put one arm out straight in front of him, holding his thumb up at the level of his eye line to check the furrows were straight. He then got back in the tractor and drove on. He looked totally absorbed and truly contented! For Lee, this was success.

It is not our job, nor is it possible, to decide what will make our children happy and successful. It is our job to give them the confidence to go out and find that happiness and success for themselves and to be unafraid to reach for their dreams.

But isn't that the job of schools too?

Before we go on to talk about how to nurture life-confidence in your children, I want to take a look at what part our schools are playing in developing this all-important quality.

Chapter 2

Revealed! The Part Schools Play

What Do Schools Teach Us?

Paradigms are habits; they are the way we have been conditioned to think from an early age. The problem is they are often in the form of limiting beliefs and the cause of low self-esteem and a negative self-image.

To live a truly happy, confident and successful life a person needs to be rounded and have a balance of the physical, social, emotional, mental, and spiritual needs. But if you think schools are adequately addressing this balance then you can think again! They're not!

Schools equip our children with knowledge, but they do not fully nurture their self-belief so that they can use that knowledge with confidence and to best effect in order to live the life they love.

In my experience this is where our education system falls short. How we think has a direct correlation with how we feel, and how we feel will influence the results we get in our lives. In schools however, the emphasis is first and foremost on academic results and league tables and the fact is – there's just not enough time in the school day for much else.

Some schools may go some way towards taking care of the emotional wellbeing of children, but in the majority of cases it stops there. Building life-confidence in our children is sadly neglected.

There is a very important point being missed here and it's this:

 Time spent on developing social and emotional skills is indeed time well spent because, ironically, studies have shown that high emotional competence has a positive, direct effect on academic achievement[2]

It has to be said that this is emphatically not a reflection on our teachers. They do a superb job of educating the adults of the future and they do it with a dedication and tirelessness that no other profession can beat.

They are, however, restricted by the system. They are dictated to by the government which has yet to go a long way before it gets the balance right between social, emotional, mental and spiritual intelligence.

So where does that leave you, the parent? Well, firstly, I'm happy to say things are beginning to change. Just as there has been a move in our schools towards healthy eating i.e. food for the body, so also are social and emotional aspects of child-development i.e. 'food for the mind', slowly beginning to seep into the system. There is in fact a new Emotional Intelligence curriculum package which has just been introduced to schools even as I write this. Great news you may think.

The bad news is: At the time of writing this, at best, most primary school teachers timetable social and emotional competence lessons for just 1/30th of the week and at worst, at those frequently busy times, it gets left out altogether.

Sadly, in addition to this, the lack of teacher training in The Three C's, which I talked about earlier, is a clear indication that the subject is not treated seriously enough and given the importance it deserves.

Independent schools fare better of course, not least because of their smaller class numbers, but as with state schools, some will be better than others.

---

[2]"Emotional Intelligence and College Success: A Research-Based Assessment and Intervention Model" Gary R. Low PhD, Darwin B. Nelson PhD

I believe there will come a day when there will be a Life-Coach in every school, employed as a permanent member of staff, just as every school has a school administrator. However, in general there is a long way to go before sufficient time and money is built into the system for this important area. So for the moment, like it or not, where your child's emotional development is concerned, the ball is firmly in your court.

 Never underestimate the importance of your job as a parent. Make no mistake about it – it is crucial.

Too often parents hand over the early education of their children completely to the school, in the belief that they don't need to do anything. How wrong they are! No one has such a perfect opportunity as you to ensure your child's success by developing his Emotional Intelligence.

When you subtract lunch time and break times, children are in contact with their teachers for around 1/5th of a 24 hour day, during which time they are often getting around a mere 1/30th of the teacher's attention!

On the other hand, they are in contact with you for probably the same amount of time each school day, but in addition to this there is the opportunity for them to be with you for a large part of the weekend and all through the holidays and, what's more, they are not competing against 30 other children – they can have one-to-one attention!

 If you want your children to grow up into confident, happy, balanced adults in this world of negativity – with all its temptations and challenges – there has never been a greater need for you to play a bigger part in making sure that happens – and no one has a better opportunity than you.

Looking at the bigger picture – our children really are the future of this planet so there is no other job more important than parenting.

Feeling daunted? Don't be. You already have a multitude of natural skills and abilities as a parent and the very fact that you are reading this now means that you recognise the importance of your role and are ready and willing to do what it takes to improve. So you've already got a head start.

By now, if you are serious about improving, you will be ready to study, digest and hopefully begin to put things in place to embark on your own journey of positive thinking and life-confidence. At this point you should now be beginning to see that the very best way to help your child on their journey to becoming a fully functioning, happy, life-confident person is to immerse yourself in the process and take that journey alongside them.

In order to work on the following concepts with your children, you need to be working on your own limiting beliefs at the same time.

So how do you go about it? Well that's what the rest of this book is all about. You are about to have the tools and know-how to be the BEST person and the BEST parent you can be!

The good news is, to help your children on the road to high Emotional Intelligence (see Part 4) and the resulting life-confidence which that brings, you don't need to be setting aside extra time in an already busy day. This is more about adopting an approach in your everyday interaction with your children which nurtures their self-esteem and sense of self-worth. It's about learning 'a way of being' with your children which is integrated into everyday life.

And it's never too late to start.

If you put in the action and apply these concepts on a regular daily basis until they become second nature to you, your children will, without a doubt, be well on the way to becoming life-confident adults with all the other life-fulfilling attributes which that brings.

Chapter 3

Introducing The B.E.S.T. Success Formula: The Four Pillars of Life-Confidence

There are four pivotal areas of development which are of crucial importance in building confidence and have a direct correlation with how happy and successful you are in life – and with children it's no exception.

These four areas together make up The B.E.S.T. Success Formula which embraces both a way of being and a way of doing.

If you apply the principles of this formula consistently and diligently, you will get in touch with your true-self and I guarantee your confidence will positively soar – and so will your child's!

The first three of these areas concerns your all-important inner emotional world, and the last one your outer world.

It is no coincidence that the balance is weighted towards what goes on in your mind. This is the one thing that you have absolute control over, and when you change the way you think, you will automatically change the way you act and the results you get in your life will change too!

Also, there's an interesting bonus: How you react to the world around you, will influence the way the world acts towards you!

In keeping with the acronym I shall introduce each component of The B.E.S.T. Success Formula in order. It could be argued that a better 'sequence' might be S.B.E.T. but it doesn't sound as good! Joking aside however, you will quickly realise that, whilst each part is indispensible to the achievement of success, by their very nature, the qualities are interdependent and are developed simultaneously. You may find though that you have a greater need to develop one specific area. My dominant area was Self-Love. Having grown up being acutely aware of what others might be thinking of me, my challenge was to dare to relax and risk letting people see the true me. I have been using this success formula for many years and I can tell you – it works.

Like all powerful concepts, The B.E.S.T. Success Formula is based on simple common sense, but although it's simple (and absolutely achievable) it's not always easy! The reason it's not easy is it needs persistence. Things won't change overnight and, as with all new ideas, we can start off with great enthusiasm and determination but somehow life gets in the way and we begin to wane, and before we know it we're back to square one. It's important therefore that you embrace the concepts until they become a habit; a way of life.

When you do – the rewards will be PRICELESS.

So without more ado let's get going. . .

PART 2

The First Pillar of

Life-Confidence:

elief

"Within you right now is the power to do things you never dreamed possible, and this power becomes available to you just as soon as you can change your beliefs"

Maxwell Maltz

Chapter 4

About Belief

Building Your Belief in Yourself
Building Your Belief in Your Child

By the word belief I don't mean religious belief. Whilst undoubtedly for many people, a religious faith can be a powerful force in helping them on their journey towards life-confidence, 'belief' in this context means self-belief.

The strength of our confidence, and therefore the quality of our life and the results we get, are directly related to our inner belief system. It follows then that boosting your child's confidence is about helping him develop a strong belief in his own abilities. In order to help him build this self-belief you must do two things, which I'm going to talk about next. Firstly you must develop belief in yourself and your ability as a parent, and secondly you must truly believe in your child.

Building Your Belief in Yourself

"Whatever the mind can conceive and believe. . . it can achieve"

Napoleon Hill

The above quote is such a powerful one.

Putting it another way: Whatever you desire in life, if it is humanly possible and your belief is strong enough, you can achieve it. The sky's the limit!

Let's stay with this for a minute:

"Anything you can *conceive...*"

When you think of something you want to do, the very fact that you have conceived the idea in the first place means it is humanly possible for you to do it. In other words you wouldn't be saying to yourself "I want to grow wings and fly to the moon!" This is fantasy. (By the way, if you're thinking thoughts like this then I'm definitely not the person to help you!)

Neither would you be saying, "I want to win the 100 metre hurdle race in the next Olympics" if you were 90 years old and walking with two sticks (the flat race maybe! – let's keep positive here!)

The point I'm making is this – if you haven't, a) the physical ability to do something, and b) enough time left in your lifetime to acquire that ability, it ain't gonna happen! So therefore you won't *conceive* of the idea in the first place.

However – assuming you are physically capable and you have time on your side then your state of mind is something else...

"Anything you can... *believe...*" Now that's a different ball game.

Let's suppose you say to yourself, "I want to be ace at public speaking" and let's assume you are physically capable and have the time left to learn the skills (or, as we've said, you wouldn't have conceived the idea in the first place). Now here's the thing:

If you don't have the belief in your ability to do it, it will never happen. As Henry Ford put it, *"Whether you think you can or whether you think you can't ... you're right"*

In other words, your ability to do something is dependent on whether you think yourself capable of doing it. This is about believing in your ability to achieve **anything** – whatever you want in life.

As human beings we all have moments when we doubt our ability to achieve something or to cope with a situation, and with parenting it's no exception. However, when you have strong self-belief, you are able to call upon that inner strength to deal with anything that comes your way.

Whether you are expecting your first baby or you're a new parent with all the associated stresses of caring for a newborn baby; whether you have an undisciplined child, a child who is struggling at school or a child who is finding difficulty with relationships; whatever the problem, there are many pot-holes along the road of bringing up children which are a challenge to our belief in our ability to cope.

Indeed, whether you are a parent, a teacher, or any other adult who plays a responsible role in the life of a child, you will have experienced moments of self-doubt. The truth is we are all human.

Firstly it's important to accept that you won't get through life without making mistakes. Neither should you want to, because it's through our mistakes that we grow. So when you make what, in your opinion, is a mistake, don't beat yourself up or you will only disempower yourself. Instead, if you look upon mistakes as opportunities to learn and grow, you will be empowered by them.

Secondly, remember that children are very resilient and forgiving, so when you make a mistake don't dwell on all the 'shoulds' and 'shouldn'ts' – admit that you got it wrong, learn from the experience then let go and move on.

Using the tools in this book to tap into your own potential and build your own self-belief will put you in a much better position to learn from your mistakes and to help your child do the same, and you will be demonstrating a positive, responsible attitude for them to emulate.

Building Your Belief in Your Child

"Whether you think they can or whether you think they can't ... you're right!"

By this I mean if you convey doubt in your child's abilities she will pick up on this and her own self-doubt will kick in, hampering her progress.

You have to believe – truly believe – in your child's innate potential.

A statement of the obvious? Maybe, yet one which is so often overlooked and rarely truly demonstrated.

Throughout this book there are a great many tips and strategies you can use to help your child to build her confidence, but unless you truly believe in her potential, and you demonstrate that belief at every available opportunity, they will have little long-term effect. Children are very perceptive and they will quickly sense a lack of sincerity.

I talk later about the importance of helping your child to call on past strengths. I am eternally grateful to the people in my life who have praised and encouraged me and shown their belief in me – my sister Chris being one of them. Even now I call on the strength of her belief in me and it's still a boost to my confidence even though she's not with me now.

So your belief in your child will have a knock-on effect not just for now but for the rest of her life – even when you are no longer around, you will be supporting her!

Building belief is all about changing your thoughts. Maxwell Maltz was an accomplished plastic surgeon. Over the years he performed surgery on a great number of patients, all of whom had low self-esteem because of some aspect of their appearance. As he amassed many case studies he began to notice that, for a proportion of the people who came to him to change the way they looked, there was no improvement in their self-image and their confidence level remained low. This led him to realise that it's no good changing what goes on on the outside unless we also change what goes on on the inside. In other words building our confidence is primarily about the way we think. These findings prompted him to write his classic book *'Psycho-Cybernetics'* in which he talks about programming the mind to improve self-confidence (see also Chapters 12 and 18).

For many years I too tried to change what was going on inside me by changing my outward impression. My own 'plastic surgery' was metaphorical – it took the form of getting qualifications. Whatever hobby I took up I felt the need to train – from being a riding instructor and judge to taking my advanced driving test and teaching driving, and taking a variety of other exams in other hobbies in between – everything stemmed from a need to change the way I felt about myself. Of course, none of this changed me inside. I only began my journey of life-confidence when I started changing the way I was thinking.

In the following chapter I am going to talk about a concept which changed my life and also the lives of many other people I know. I guarantee it will help you to change the way you think and build that all-important belief in your child's ability.

Chapter 5

Getting Inside Your Child's Head

How Your Mind Works
A Picture of Your Mind
Your Conscious Mind
Your Sub-Conscious Mind
The Four Truths Will Set You Free!
It's Your Choice

"As a man thinketh in his heart, so is he."

Proverbs 23:7

Whilst you may want to dip in and out of the rest of this book, I strongly recommend you read this chapter to begin with because, if you truly grasp its significance, it will have a direct correlation with the success of you as a parent in building your child's confidence. As you develop your level of awareness, you will find it easy to build your belief in your child's potential and you will be far more likely to keep up your new approach until it becomes a natural habit for both you and your child.

I'm now going to introduce you to a very powerful concept. It forms the underlying foundation upon which the whole of this book has been written.

 Without realising it, whether in a positive way or a negative way, you are actually programming your child's sub-conscious mind!

That's what I'm going to talk about next!

How Your Mind Works

As with all concepts we can process information much easier if we are able to form a picture in our 'mind's eye'. Although there are plenty of pictures of the human brain, no-one has been able to create a picture of the mind because it is an abstract concept. The mind in fact permeates your whole body.

The closest we can come to picturing the mind is a diagram formulated by the late, Dr. Thurman Fleet of San Antonio, Texas in 1934 [circa]. Dr. Fleet was the founder of Concept Therapy.

I was introduced to this diagram by author and philosopher Bob Proctor (featured in *'The Secret'*) when I attended one of his inspired seminars. It made a powerful impression on me. Although this seminar was for adults, I realised that, by chance, I had stumbled upon the missing piece of the education puzzle I had been searching for.

I knew then and there I had to bring this concept to children.

The more I thought about it the more excited I became! I am now going to pass this information on to you – to pass on to your children when they are old enough to understand it.

If you really study this, you will open your mind to a whole new world of possibilities, both for yourself and for your children and that all important belief and expectation will be cemented.

 Everything I talk about in this book will be enhanced by your understanding of what follows next.

A Picture of Your Mind

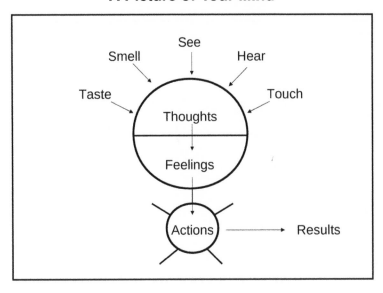

Courtesy Bob Proctor – LifeSuccess Productions

In this diagram, the large circle represents your mind, the small one – your body.

Your mind is made up of 2 parts:

1. Your conscious, thinking mind where all your thoughts are formed.

2. Your sub-conscious mind where your feelings and emotions are evoked.

Thoughts are made up of interpretations of past or present experiences and are influenced by people you meet, words you hear, things you read or see in the media etc.

Your Conscious Mind

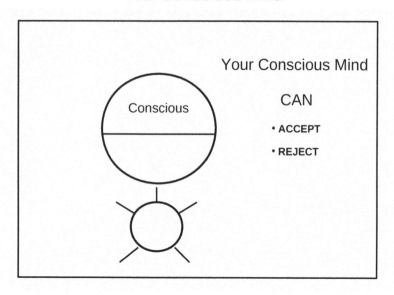

Courtesy Bob Proctor – LifeSuccess Productions

You have the ability to choose to accept or reject thoughts which come into your conscious mind.

The problem is, for most of the time we are not truly thinking! We are off guard and we are unaware of what we are allowing to enter our minds. This is the danger time! It is during this time – when the mind is on 'automatic pilot' – that we allow ourselves to absorb a great many of the negative thoughts, ideas and information about ourselves from the world around us.

Your Sub-Conscious Mind

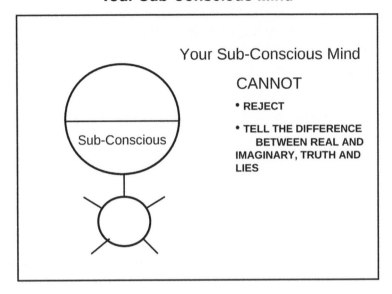

Courtesy Bob Proctor – LifeSuccess Productions

Your Sub-Conscious Mind is like your own internal 'Genie'. It's your mind's centre of power which turns thoughts into actions. And here's the key: Unlike your conscious mind, your sub-conscious mind *cannot* reject what is fed into it, it can only accept it – whether it's truth or fiction!

This is the most important piece of information you will ever hear. In fact, it's so important that I'm going to repeat it...

 Your sub-conscious mind cannot reject what is fed into it, it can only accept it – whether it's truth or fiction!

When a thought or idea is repeated often enough, it becomes lodged in your sub-conscious mind. And once your sub-conscious mind has accepted it, you cannot help but to act on it! That thought is automatically transmuted into action.

In the diagram, the body is deliberately smaller than the mind. This is because the mind is the master. A thought triggers a bio-chemical response and your body simply has to act out what your sub-conscious mind is telling it.

To summarise – here are four important truths:

"The Four Truths Will Set You Free!"

1. Your conscious mind can accept or reject any idea which comes along. You have a choice as to what you allow yourself to think.

2. Your sub-conscious mind has no such choice. It can only accept everything which is fed to it by the conscious mind.

3. Your sub-conscious mind cannot differentiate between truth and lies; good and bad.

4. Once an idea has taken root in your sub-conscious mind through constant repetition, you simply have to act on it – and the corresponding results will show up in your life!

Please read those four truths a few times. As you work through this book you will begin to really get a feel for the power of them, and their relevance to building your own self-belief and the self-belief of your child. If you really get the implications of this you will see how exciting it is.

Are you ready for another bombshell?

Here it comes. . .

 You have a power within you that is stronger than any challenge you will ever come across and so have your children!

Let me tell you, when I first realised this I was so excited I had sleepless nights for a WEEK! Now before you read any further, re-read the Four Truths, but this time apply them to your child:

1. Your child's conscious mind can accept or reject any idea which comes along. Your child has a choice as to what he allows himself to think.

2. Your child's sub-conscious mind has no such choice. It can only accept everything which is fed to it by the conscious mind.

3. Your child's sub-conscious mind cannot differentiate between truth and lies; good and bad.

4. Once an idea has taken root in your child's sub-conscious mind through constant repetition, she or he simply has to act on it – and the corresponding results will show up in your child's life!

How powerful is that!

It's Your Choice

To believe in the potential of your children you must be able to recognise your own potential. You can be an enormous inspiration to them. You are unique. You are a mass of vibrating energy. It has been said that if the energy in one person's body could be harnessed it could be used to light up an entire city for a week! Whilst I can't vouch for the accuracy of that, we have certainly all heard of the person who in an emergency turns 'super human' and is able to lift a car single-handedly by tapping into reserved energy sources.

We have a HUGE amount of untapped energy – and we moan about how tired we feel!

Believe me – you have such awesome potential within you. And so has your child. The question is "When are you going to use it?"

Just think about the following scenario for a minute:

It's Sunday evening and you are suffering from 'Sunday Evening Syndrome' – i.e. you know you have to go to work the next day, you feel the evening will be nearly gone and you feel tired and stressed just thinking about it.

In fact from early evening onwards you can think of nothing else and your weekend has ended prematurely! Even if you don't have a job at present I'm sure you can relate to that feeling.

Now imagine you receive a phone call from work to say that due to a breakdown in the heating system, the office will be closed until Tuesday.

Immediately, a huge weight is lifted from your shoulders. Suddenly – you feel alive! Miraculously – you are no longer tired! In fact you now feel the night is young and you may even start to plan where to go for the evening!

So what happened then to change you from that low energy state, to feeling on top of the world? You are still physically the same person you were a minute ago before the phone rang. Nothing has changed there.

What has changed is your state of mind – the way you choose to think. And all that latent energy surges into your body simply because you choose to think positively. I use the word 'choose' deliberately. Whether we choose to think energising thoughts or whether we choose to think thoughts which will drain our energy, the choice is entirely ours.

It's no good blaming past circumstances for where you are in your life right now either! Everything that has happened in your life to bring you to where you are now, has happened as a result of your own choices! You, and only you, are responsible for your life (but that's another book!) For those of you who want to explore how to attract the circumstances you want into your life I highly recommend you watch the DVD called *'The Secret'*.

So it follows that everything that is going to happen in your child's future life will happen as a result of his own choices. His life lies open like a book with empty pages waiting to be written on.

Suffice to say, choosing to develop a positive mental attitude is crucial if we want to build belief, enthusiasm and self-love in our children and ensure they make choices which will lead them to success.

And that's what The B.E.S.T. Success Formula is all about.

OK. So let's get down to the nitty gritty: How do you apply all this knowledge to change yourself for the better and, in turn, help your child to do the same?

That's what I am going to talk about next.

Chapter 6

Your First Sign of Sanity!

The Three Stages of Consciousness

The saying goes that talking to yourself is the first sign of insanity. I say that *negative* self-talk is the first sign of insanity but *positive* self-talk is the first sign of sanity!

To help your child on the road to life-confidence, you are going to have to help them to change the voice in their head to a more positive, optimistic one, but to do this you must also practise being mindful of the voice in your own head. You know – the one which is constantly 'rabbiting' on? I mean those mind-rambling, avalanches of thought which seem to keep coming with no apparent conscious effort on your part.

First of all there are the inconsequential thoughts like,

"I wonder what we can have for dinner tonight?"

"I must ring David to find out the number of that restaurant"

Then there are the negative thoughts like,

"The car park's sure to be full this time of year"

"They're bound to have sold out of bread"

"I've just put that washing out and it looks like rain!"

"I'll bet those traffic lights will turn red just as I get to them!"

And the self deprecating thoughts like,

"I'm no good at. . ."

"I bet she thinks I'm stupid"

"I'll never be able to understand. . ."

"I'm hopeless at . . ."

And so on. You fill in the blanks.

It's this kind of thinking which subconsciously drags us down and which we need to address in order to build a strong self-confidence in any area. But, the voice in your head may seem almost impossible to switch off. At least not for long.

Although it can be quietened through meditation, in the general course of everyday life that voice is an intrinsic part of the way your mind works. However – here's the good news:

You can control what your mind-voice says by choosing the type of thoughts you allow to enter your mind.

And here's the really good news:

 When you change your thoughts – your children will begin to change their thinking too!

So here's how you do it: To re-programme your sub-conscious mind and change the way you have been conditioned to think – changing negative thoughts to positive ones and changing beliefs which inhibit, to those which empower – you will need to go through three main stages which I shall call 'The Three Stages of Consciousness'.

The Three Stages of Consciousness

Stage 1 – Awareness

Firstly, begin to notice your negative thoughts. Monitor that incessant 'Moaning Minnie', that 'Profit of Doom' inside your head. Take note of what it's saying and how many negative messages it's feeding your sub-conscious mind. Become aware not only of your negative self-talk but the disempowering beliefs you have concerning yourself and the world around you.

Secondly, an important factor in changing your inside world is the amount of depressing information you expose yourself to from outside. And remember, not only do you expose yourself to this negativity – you expose your kids to it too.

This world we bring our children into is full of gloom and doom. Actually, it's full of positive stuff too but that doesn't make 'interesting' news!

Every time they are in the room when the news is on, every time they see a newspaper lying around with some ghastly headline story, every time they watch a film or video involving aggression and violence of any kind they are sub-consciously absorbing this negative energy.

So simultaneously, whilst you are noticing your internal thoughts, begin to notice the negative messages you are bombarded with from the outside world – the TV, radio, headlines in the papers, everyday conversations with friends and family – because here's the thing: only when you become aware of it can you begin to do something about it.

In fact, put your mind on 'red alert' and develop a new level of awareness whereby you notice everything that's negative both within you and without – regularly.

Once you are fully aware of this negativity, both in your own thoughts and in the world around you, you will need to do something about it – you are now ready for stage 2.

Stage 2 – The Positive Equivalent

When you are in the habit of noticing your negative thoughts and beliefs on a regular everyday basis, you now need to stop thinking them!

Of course, this is easier said than done. The problem being: If you try just to stop thinking them it won't work. As I have already said, you can't stop that voice. If you stop thinking one negative thought and you don't replace it with anything else, you will create a space for another negative thought to enter. So when you stop the voice in your head from saying one thing, you absolutely must give it something else to say.

Now the conscious mind can only hold one thought at a time – either positive or negative.

Try this for a moment: Try thinking about something you are worried about and something which you are grateful for – both at precisely the same time. It's impossible to do.

So the trick is this:

When you think a negative thought, notice it, then immediately replace it with the positive equivalent.

I'm going to talk later about affirmations but for now here are a couple of examples:

Follow, *"The car park's sure to be full"*

by, *"There'll be a place waiting there somewhere for me, I'm relaxing and being patient"*

And, *"They're bound to be sold out of bread"*

becomes, *"But there could still be some left and anyway, it's no problem, we can eat cream crackers."*

Instead of, *"It's sure to rain just as I put the washing out"*

try saying, *"The washing could be dry by lunchtime, and if it rains it's not the end of the world. I'll cope with it!"*

And from now on start believing and expecting those traffic lights to stay green... and when they do, express your gratitude to the universe.

It is said that it takes approximately thirty days of concentrated effort for a habit to be cemented in our sub-conscious mind, so practise each stage constantly – and give it time.

When you get into the habit of regularly replacing your negative thoughts with positive ones, you are approaching Stage 3.

Stage 3 – Think Before You Think

The trick with this one is to catch your negative thoughts before you even think them. This is the stage when you have practised positive equivalents for so long you find yourself actually saying the positive equivalent before your inner voice gets the chance to say the negative!

The first two stages you have to consciously work at, but this final stage will just begin to happen without any conscious decision on your part. That's because, at last, your sub-conscious mind is beginning to take over.

And here's the amazing thing. When you are living at stage 3 level, it's like a self-fulfilling prophesy. The universal energy has a habit of giving you back what you put out. So if you expect that empty parking space it will turn up (just as conversely, if you expect not to find one – you won't!).

And remember I said the body has to do what the mind tells it to do? In other areas of your life, as you begin to think positive thoughts, you will find yourself starting to put in the necessary action to make sure those thoughts materialise.

And every time you put in the action you will be cementing those beliefs in your sub-conscious mind even more. It's that virtuous circle again!

This model is not always linear. Except for a very few highly enlightened people in the world, Stage 3 will always be concomitant with Stage 2.

In other words, whilst some thoughts will be Stage 3 ones, there will still be those negative ones which will sneak into your conscious mind when you are off guard (Stage 2), which you will need to follow up with positive equivalents.

Indeed, there will be times when you switch off altogether and enter automatic pilot mode. You then will work at Stage 1 again. (I did say it was a life's journey!)

You can't rush this. Patience is a virtue, and you must realise that to change the habits of a lifetime it takes just a bit longer than a few days or weeks. But don't be daunted.

I am reminded here of the story of the man and his mentor. It went something like this: A man was told by his mentor that if he worked hard, in 10 years time he could be a very rich man. "But I shall be 55 by then" said the man impatiently. To which the mentor replied, "How old will you be in 10 years time if you *don't* work hard?"

The moral? Begin it now! However long it takes it will be well worth the effort. Although, for an adult, it may take patience and perseverance, you can be sure of one thing: It's never too late to change.

But how is changing yourself going to help your children?

Well it's like this – as you begin to become aware of just how many thought-pattern habits you have been programmed with over the years, you will become more acutely aware of two things:

1. The importance of your part as a role model for your children.

2. What a golden opportunity you have to programme positive self-belief into their minds before their negative beliefs become too entrenched!

Are you getting a feel for what an incredibly powerful, exciting opportunity we have with the benefit of this knowledge? Are you beginning to see the picture?

If you apply everything you learn here to your own life for just 30 days, you will, without doubt, start to see and feel changes and every day will start to be an improvement on the day before.

Realistically you may have lapses when the business of everyday life takes over – that's normal. Just pick up where you left off and don't give up.

Stay with this and I guarantee you will change into a much more positive thinking person and both your life, and the lives of your children will benefit and change dramatically as a result!

I don't make promises lightly but I speak from first hand experience. I grew up with some crippling limiting beliefs. For many years I was painfully shy in the company of people whom I didn't know well. I found it hard to make conversation without stumbling over my words and I was constantly imagining people were thinking the worst of me. I got to a point where I was unable to go to social functions without first taking an over-the-counter drug to relax my nerves. Where I grew up the saying was, *"She wouldn't say 'Boo' to a goose!"*

It has taken a lot of self-discipline and determination to change my low self-esteem for the better, but – through working on the concepts I'm about to show you in this book – change it I have. . .

I am now able to stand in front of a large audience and talk with confidence. I am also becoming progressively independent of the good opinion of other people and I am true to myself and not afraid to say what I think.

I haven't tried saying 'Boo' to a goose yet, but when I do, I'll know I've truly arrived!!

Chapter 7

Paradigm Power

Useful Beliefs
Useless Beliefs
Limiting Beliefs
Are You Unconsciously Conditioning Your Baby's Mind?
The Peril Of Put-Downs

As children, we absorb many habits and beliefs which are fed to us from our parents and their parents before them. When we accept these beliefs without question they become lifelong habits and we become conditioned. Conditioned thoughts or habits which lodge in the sub-conscious are known as paradigms.

 Your thoughts and actions are the product of other people's conditioned thoughts.

Paradigms are passed from generation to generation, conditioning the sub-conscious mind.

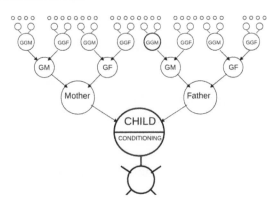

Not all beliefs are bad of course. A portion of them are useful, but others serve no useful purpose whatsoever and the worst beliefs are the totally disempowering ones which severely limit our potential, often for the rest of our lives.

Here are some examples:

Useful Beliefs

Beliefs which fall into this category are commonsense beliefs based on facts, which keep us safe and healthy, like,

- "You need to look both ways before crossing the road"
- "If you swim in the sea when the tide is going out you may get swept away by the current"
- "Smoking is bad for you"

Useless Beliefs

These are trivial beliefs or beliefs based on superstition or 'Old Wives' Tales'

- "If you walk under a ladder you will have bad luck"
- "You will never make a good cup of tea if you don't warm the teapot first"

Here are some more examples of useless beliefs:

Example 1

There's the story of the person who, for many years, always cut both ends off a joint of ham before putting it into the oven. When asked why she did this she said it was because her mother had always done it, and her mother had done it because she had seen *her* mother do it. Finally when the grandmother was asked why she cut the ends off her ham she said that she had done it to make it fit the shape of her roasting tin!

Example 2

When cooking runner beans, I always used to cut them into long thin slices along the length of the bean. I continued this habit for many years until, when visiting a friend, I noticed she cut her beans diagonally into diamond shapes. I had never given the matter a moment's thought before then, but I finally realised I was mindlessly copying my mother and her mother and most likely her mother's mother! (Problem is, I'm now into another habit of cutting my beans into diamonds!)

Example 3

When peeling a banana my mother would always make us throw away the part at the very end which had black in the centre. She said, *"That's the bit where all the germs are"*! And even though I know it's ludicrous, when I'm not thinking I still throw away that black bit to this day! Old habits die hard!

I'm sure you will have stories of your own to tell about old habits and 'Old Wives' Tales' which have been passed down from generation to generation. Maybe you'll start to become aware of ones you hadn't noticed before. Habits which serve no useful purpose but ones which are pretty harmless.

However, it's the next category of beliefs which are the dangerous ones – both for you and your children. These have been stunting our growth, crushing our confidence and suppressing our potential for most of our adult lives, and they're called 'Limiting Beliefs'.

Limiting Beliefs

Limiting beliefs are those self-deprecating beliefs we have about our own abilities and circumstances which limit our progress and inhibit our personal growth.

They are crippling, and the quicker you start working on eliminating them from your mind, the quicker you will move forward with your life, and the quicker you will help your child to move forward as a result.

With limiting beliefs you should take yourself through the same three stages of consciousness and when it comes to thinking the positive equivalent, always remember –

You don't have to believe the thought you are planting. Your sub-conscious mind will accept anything you tell it if you repeat it often enough. The paradox is you will then begin to believe it!

Here are some examples of changing our limiting beliefs:

"I'm useless at remembering names"

becomes: *"I have a brilliant memory for names"*

"I'm going to be so nervous when I give that speech"

becomes: *"I am confident I can give a great speech"*

"I'm no good at talking to people"

becomes: *"I am getting better at talking to people"*

"I'm so weak when it comes to resisting chocolate"

becomes: *"My will power is becoming stronger every day"*

and so on.

It's important to imagine the 'new you' as vividly as possible when you are making these positive statements about yourself. Don't just pay 'lip service' to the words without getting emotionally involved (see the section on Affirmations in Chapter 12).

Our children's paradigms so often take the form of limiting beliefs, and limiting beliefs cause a lack of confidence. But how do they get these beliefs? Of course, no normal parent would knowingly programme their child's mind with limiting beliefs... but what about unknowingly?

It all starts when a new life begins:

Are You Unconsciously Conditioning Your Baby's Mind?

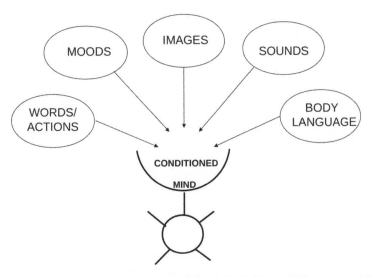

A YOUNG BABY'S MIND IS WIDE OPEN TO OTHER PEOPLE'S
MOODS, BODY LANGUAGE, WORDS AND ACTIONS,
SOUNDS AND IMAGES

The above diagram illustrates just how vulnerable the young mind is to being conditioned by external stimuli.

From our earliest years we have been taking thoughts, images and ideas from the outside world into our sub-conscious mind. In fact, as a young baby we do not have the ability to make a conscious choice, our mind is wide open to absorbing things directly into the sub-conscious.

In addition, we are all born with the primitive instinct to do what it takes to avoid rejection from 'the tribe'. As a child we copy our elders in order to be accepted within the family.

In the early years we are eager to please our parents (the leaders of the tribe) and we are very aware of the expectations they have of us.

We will always strive to live up to those expectations (even though they may often take the form of limiting beliefs). We copy the same actions, use the same language and adopt the same belief system, and by the age of five that belief system is firmly established.

At school we strive to be accepted as part of 'the school tribe' and when we join 'the teenage tribe' we have a very strong need to conform, look cool, wear the latest fashion, adopt the same language, hang out in the same places, and generally do the same things.

As we carry our limiting beliefs about ourselves into adulthood, they become cemented and we gravitate towards the people and circumstances which reinforce those beliefs. We join 'the adult tribe' which best reflects the way we are – the one we feel most comfortable with – and the pattern is set.

The Peril of Put-Downs

The image we have of ourselves, plays an important part in the development of our confidence, and our self-image is formed by the feedback we get from others.

Even when spoken in jest, phrases like, *"You're so clumsy", "You're always forgetting things", "You're so slow"*, will have a lasting impact upon your child's self-image and, in turn, their life-confidence.

What's more, put-downs are even more damaging when a child overhears us talking about him to someone else. As a teacher I see it all the time. It's very common for parents to discuss their children whilst they are present:

"He finds maths really difficult"

"She's really struggling with her reading"

"She's so forgetful"

"He's very shy" etc.

The impact that these throw-away negative statements can have on a child's self-esteem is immeasurable.

Well-meaning parents, carers and grandparents, and later, authority figures such as teachers and youth workers, who are all doing the best job they know how, usually have no idea just how strong an influence they have on the formation of a child's self-image.

They may unwittingly make negative comments which lodge in the young impressionable mind and, based on such comments and ideas, the child's self-image is gradually formed.

Once the seed of a limiting belief has been sown, a young child will then be 'tuned in' to notice stimuli from the outside world, which validate those thoughts he has been conditioned to think. With repetition, these thoughts, images and ideas are consolidated in the sub-conscious mind and eventually become habits or paradigms which he acts out.

Here's an example for you:

A little girl drops something on the floor and her mum says, *"You're so clumsy!"*. Unless she has a strong sense of self-worth and self-confidence she will take that comment to heart, or rather 'to sub-conscious'.

If she already has negative beliefs about herself, in future, that little girl will begin to notice every time she fumbles or drops something or doesn't get it right first time. Limiting beliefs about being clumsy will be fed into her sub-conscious mind again and again until they are firmly cemented. Remember whatever we allow into our sub-conscious mind we have to act on? Well, she will believe she is clumsy and hey-ho, the body being the servant of the mind, she will begin to behave in a clumsy manner from then on!

This habitual way of thinking and acting will, more than likely, stay with her for the rest of her life... and all because of one careless remark!

Once formed, the image we have of ourselves is strongly cemented over the years and it takes much persistence and patience to change our old conditioning for the better.

Of course. as I have said, it's never too late to change – I am living proof of that. Usually however, the longer the idea has been there, the more it is entrenched into your sub-conscious, the more you have to work at it and the longer it takes to change it.

To summarise:

 If the wrong negative messages are fed into a child's mind from an early age, that child will grow up with a negative self-belief which is firmly entrenched into the psyche.

This all sounds like gloom and doom doesn't it? It needn't be. In fact if you are the sort of person who says the glass is half full instead of half empty then you will see that this coin can be flipped around and used to great advantage! Substitute the word positive for negative and you are reminded of the crucial message of this book, namely,

 If the right positive *messages are fed into the young impressionable mind, how much easier it is to develop life-confidence from an early age rather than later when a life time of limiting beliefs have to first be eliminated!*

Please read the above statement again to lodge it into your sub-conscious. As child carers, what a powerful and privileged position we are in!

Of course children will hear comments made about them by others as they grow up. But if we have done, and continue to do, our job well, they will have a strong enough belief in themselves not to take those comments too seriously.

Armed with this knowledge, what a fantastic opportunity we have as parents to ensure young minds are programmed in such a positive way as to have a positive effect on their confidence – for the rest of their lives.

What a head start we can give them!

⚠ *If, at this stage, you are thinking "All this is pretty obvious" BEWARE! It may be obvious, but it is one thing knowing about something and quite another putting it into action, and I am willing to bet you have plenty of room for improvement in the way you interact with your children – we all have.*

OK. So much for dealing with the negativity which comes from us, but what about dealing with the things we are fed from the outside world? Surely that's out of our control?

Actually you have more control over those 'outside forces' than you may think you have:

Chapter 8

Beware of Those Outside Forces

Turn Off That TV! – Control That Computer!
Choosing the People You Mix With

From the time we get up in the morning to the time we go to bed at the end of the day, whether we like it or not, we are bombarded with negative energy. The content of the daily news illustrates what a negative society we live in. No one, it seems, wants to hear about happily married couples, neighbours who are the best of friends, people who are living happy healthy lives, or communities who are living in harmony.

But we don't choose the content of the newspapers, television soaps, radio programmes, magazines, films, DVDs, videos… or do we? Actually, if there were enough positive-thinking people in the world the content of all media genre would change overnight, because negativity just wouldn't sell!

For now though, at least for our lifetime and maybe that of our children and our children's children, like it or not, we are stuck with a world of environmental pollution, global warming, racial hatred, wars, terrorist attacks, murders and famine, and try as we may, it's impossible to go through life without reading or hearing about these things. However, whilst we can't change our outside world, we can change our inside world by choosing what information we allow ourselves and our children to absorb from outside.

In other words, choosing what we allow ourselves to dwell on.

And here's the thing –

 If enough people worked on changing their inside world, our outside one would change too!

When watching or listening to the news headlines choose the news you want to listen to, flicking to another channel in between news items. Read the newspapers less often or not at all. I freely admit it is many years now since I read a newspaper from cover to cover. I normally keep up to date with current affairs by listening to the news headlines or catching glimpses of them in newsagents. I am very selective with what I allow myself to listen to or read in greater depth and if I miss some dramatic event you can bet your life there will always be plenty of people to tell me about it!

If you are taken off guard and you hear or see something negative which starts to take a grip on your imagination, switch your thoughts to something pleasurable or think of all the good things there are in the world to be grateful for, or do something physically active to change your state of mind.

Turn Off That TV! – Control That Computer!

Of course it's neither realistic nor desirable for children to be shielded obsessively from everything bad that goes on in the world around them. But let's at least start to think about addressing the balance.

I'm not suggesting you should rush out and dump the television! But be selective. Unsupervised television viewing for young children is bad news. Plan what you are going to watch and what you allow your children to watch. The same goes for electronic games.

You may be already making sure your children don't overhear too many negative things and you are already mindful of what they watch on the television and the games they play, but if you are applying this to yourself as well, it will be more than doubly effective.

Young children are no fools. If a violent episode comes on the television, by the time you get to the remote control to switch stations, they've already seen enough, and you have drawn attention to the very thing you don't want them to see. Much better to not have that programme on in the first place.

Firstly you will be doing yourself a favour, and secondly you will be a good role model for your children.

When you restrict a child from doing something be sure to replace it with other options which are equally or even more enjoyable.

Whilst it's not the purpose of this book to go over ways to solve specific behaviour problems, suffice to say – the positive equivalent is a useful way of offsetting any bad habit and can be used to good effect with all children in many situations.

For example, after making it clear when and how long television time is going to be from now on, encourage your children to take part in the discussion process of forming new habits and rules, and building replacement fun things like games, clubs, having friends round, story time, dog-walking, baking time etc. into the daily/weekly timetable. For more ideas on ways to occupy your children have a look at my ebook "Boredom Busters For Kids".

It is so easy to go for the quiet life and allow your child to sit in front of a television or computer screen all evening. You may have convinced yourself that children are not affected by violence if it is in the form of an animated game or fiction, but there are many who would disagree. Although research is ongoing there is some suggestion that exposure to violence on television and in video games increases physiological arousal and aggression-related thoughts, feelings and behaviour, both in children and young adults. Being programmed with negativity on a repetitive basis can be an energy drainer and is likely to affect your child's mental attitude. It is certainly a de-sensitiser.

 ROLE MODEL: To counterbalance all the negativity our children are fed each day then, they need to be surrounded by plenty of positivity, and the person who is best placed to feed them that positivity is you. It all begins with working on your

*own positive mental attitude (PMA). If you don't
want your children to absorb too much negativity,
make sure they don't see you absorbing it!*

Choosing the People You Mix With

The people you interact with on a daily basis can be another energy drainer. This is an interesting one as you may not even be aware of the amount of negativity you absorb from other people each day.

Financial author Robert Allen states that our income matches the average income of the 5 people in our life whom we spend the most time with. Substitute 'beliefs and aspirations' for the word 'income' and you arrive at a statement which is equally true but is potentially cause for much greater concern. I say potentially because of course it could equally be cause for much celebration, depending solely on who you mix with.

Take a moment to write down the names of the 5 people who you spend most of your time with. When you are next with these people start to notice the language they use. Are they mainly positive people or negative? Do they see the glass as half full or half empty? Do they see the good in other people or are they always gossiping? Do they make the best of things or do they criticise, blame, and complain?

 *Notice when a friend starts moaning and
complaining about something (usually you won't
have long to wait!). Count the negative statements
they make. Then notice yourself agreeing and
joining in! Now realise you are holding a mirror up
to yourself!*

It's a salutary 'light bulb' moment!

Notice how easily you slip in to talking in the same vein. It's a habit of a lifetime based on the primitive desire to be accepted within 'the tribe'. It's in our genes, and every time we do it we are cementing our limiting beliefs about ourselves and the world around us.

So how do you change?

I'm not going to suggest you drop all your old friends – the trick is to see them less often and, when you do, don't feed their negativity – dare to disagree.

> **ACTION: Next time you hear a negative comment which you don't agree with, instead of nodding and letting it pass, practise daring to disagree and see what happens.**

Often when you disagree with someone they change their tack and begin to backtrack and start agreeing with you! It's that desire to be part of the tribe.

At the same time as limiting time with negative friends begin to foster new friendships with more positive minded people to bring more of a balance into your life. It will make a huge difference to your outlook on life and remember, you are doing this not just for yourself but for your children. What better motivation can you have than that!

Chapter 9

BEWARE! Little Words With Big Meanings

The Power of 'No'
'Don't' Do This!
'But' – The Great Eraser
The Invisible 'But'

The Power of 'No'

I remember my mum telling me proudly that the very first word I ever spoke was "No" and a long emphatic "Noooooo!" at that! In fact, like me, one of the very first words many babies learn to say is the word "No".

In his book *"What to Say When You Talk to Yourself"* Shad Helmstetter writes: "During the first eighteen years of our lives, if we grew up in fairly average, reasonably positive homes, we were told *"No!"* or what we could not do, more than 148,000 times!. . . the "yes's" we received simply didn't balance out the "no's".

Children hear a myriad of negative messages every day and if a parent is constantly saying 'No', how can the child be expected to differentiate between the habitual trivial 'No's and the more crucial ones?

⚠ *Beware of the overuse of the word 'No' with young children. For the 'No's to have the greatest impact, they should be reserved for the things that really matter.*

How much more powerful is the word 'No' when it is reserved only for the important things.

From the time they learn to walk children are natural risk-takers. They fall down – they get up – they fall down – they get up – again and again. Gradually, as they get older, children become more self-conscious and less willing to have a go for fear of failure.

To develop their self-confidence, it is so important that we encourage our children to 'have a go' at things and to praise their attempts.

Here's an example: When tidying up, your child is carrying several puzzles precariously perched on top of one another and they topple and fall.

You can either say something like,

> "No don't do that they'll fall. . . now look what you've done! That was silly to try and carry them all at once!"

or you can say,

> "Whoops! Never mind. That was a good try. Next time it might be best to just carry one at a time"

Which of those will undermine their confidence and which will boost it? Which will encourage them to take risks and which will inhibit them? The second one is of course the more encouraging approach.

Unfortunately we play a large part in fostering inhibition in our children and we aren't even aware we're doing it! From a very young age we are constantly sending negative messages to our kids with such phrases as: *"Be careful!" "Mind you don't fall!" "Don't touch that!" "Don't go near there!" "You'll hurt yourself!" "You'll fall!" "You'll get lost!"* etc.

Combine these with the negative messages that children receive from the media, television, videos and people around them, and is it any wonder that, as they grow up, they start to view the world as a dangerous place to be and hold back for fear of failure?

On the subject of saying 'No' I was talking to a friend the other day about her grandchildren who are aged one and three. She told me that 'No' was a banned word in their household and that it was always replaced by an explanation of why it wasn't a good idea to do a certain thing.

Wow! To appreciate what an achievement that is, just try to go for one day without saying the word 'No' to a toddler!

Of course we need to protect our kids from dangers, but keep those No's to a minimum.

'Don't' Do This!

Close your eyes for a minute and try the following exercise:

You are allowed to think of absolutely anything you wish but, whatever other thoughts come into your mind, don't think of a blue elephant!

As soon as I say don't think of something what do you immediately do? You think of it. Right?

It reminds me of one of the 'Brer Rabbit' stories by Enid Blyton. When Brer Rabbit is caught by Brer Fox he says something like, *"I don't care what you do with me Brer Fox, but please don't throw me into that bramble bush".* Of course Brer Fox does just that, which is exactly what Brer Rabbit wants him to do! Being a rabbit he happily dives into the bush and down into a rabbit hole! Brer Rabbit knew the power of the word 'don't'!

I remember playing a game with my children at bedtime when I wanted to get them off to sleep. Instead of saying, *"Hurry up and get to sleep"* (meaning *"**Don't** stay awake"*), I would say, *"See who can keep their eyes open the longest!"* It worked like a dream – literally! Trying to stay awake meant they were asleep and dreaming much quicker than if they had tried to go to sleep!

 As well as cutting down the word 'No' from your vocabulary, beware of the over-use of the word 'Don't'.

With very young children when we focus unnecessarily on what we don't want them to do we are often inadvertently encouraging them to do it by drawing attention to it. *'Don't'* is a very powerful word: *"Don't walk in that puddle" "Don't run away" "Don't touch that" "Don't put your feet on the chair" "Don't, don't, don't!"*

I saw a mother once with a little toddler. They were sitting near a radiator and in a very firm voice the mother said, *"Now don't go near that radiator. It's hot"*

Until the mother had pointed it out, the toddler had not been the least bit interested in the radiator. But now, of course, it had become a huge fascination! What a wonderful game! Run up to the radiator and pretend to touch it and watch mum's face as she gets madder and madder! *"I've found the 'Control-Your-Mum' button!"*

For the next 10 minutes a battle ensued culminating in the exasperated mum getting up and taking the toddler to another part of the room!

This stressful battle of wills could easily have been avoided by distracting the child and not drawing attention to the radiator, or better still, not sitting near the radiator in the first place! Of course children need to be told that radiators are hot, and often they need to learn the hard way, but using that word 'don't' is like giving them an invitation.

On the basis that children give us more of what we focus on, it makes sense to focus on the good things. They will always do what gets them the most attention. All too often, however, we see parents taking more notice of badly behaved children than their well behaved peers or siblings. It's such an easy trap to fall into.

If we dwell on the bad and ignore the good, what message does this convey? Right! *"You can get more attention if you're naughty"* – bringing the incentive to be good down to zero!

When getting a class of thirty children to co-operate, the negative approach would be an uphill battle. If I walk into a classroom of noisy children and say *"Stop talking!"* (meaning 'Don't' talk), I might as well speak to the wall.

If, on the other hand, if I say something like,

"Well done Laura and Rachel you're working so sensibly"

or *"Thank you all those children who are sitting quietly, you are such a help to me!"*

It's like flicking a switch! The noise drops immediately!

Try it with your children. If one of them is misbehaving try taking your attention to the other one and commenting on how good they are.

But don't just say, *"Thomas is a good boy"* Instead, target your praise and say something like, *"Thank you for walking so sensibly Thomas. That's such a help to me"*.

This way, you're subtly pointing out to the misbehaving child the sort of behaviour that will get your attention. Then make sure you use positive reinforcement by giving them lots of attention when they are good.

These strategies are simple yet very powerful. However it takes practice. It's so easy to fall into the trap of reacting to bad behaviour – we all do it. Try applying the three levels of awareness mentioned earlier. First be on the alert. Start to become increasingly aware of your reactions and notice when your attention is drawn to the bad behaviour. Then practise stopping yourself each time you begin to give your attention to the naughty child and make a concerted effort to reinforce any good behaviour with praise.

This is an ongoing discipline which has to be constantly worked at. The main thing is to remain calm. If your child manages to get an emotional reaction from you for his inappropriate behaviour then he's won that round, but keep at it and you will eventually begin to see positive results.

'But' – The Great Eraser

⚠ *'But' is another word which can either empower or disempower, purely depending on when you say it!*

Have you ever thought about the position of the word 'but' in a sentence?

Take the following two examples when commenting on a child's work:

Example 1

*"It's interesting, **but** you've made lots of spelling mistakes!"*

Example 2

*"Great! Just one or two spelling mistakes, **but** this is a really interesting piece of work!"*

(see also 'The Feedback Sandwich' in Chapter 10)

Notice two things about these examples:

Firstly, our attention always goes to the 'but' phrase, i.e. the last part of the sentence. The word 'but' always diminishes anything that is said before it and focuses the attention on the words that come after it. It is therefore important to put the positive part of the sentence last.

Secondly, in consciously putting the positive statement after the word 'but', the speaker becomes more aware of the emphasis and automatically plays down the negative and emphasises the positive by adding superlatives as I have done.

In addition, beginning the sentence in a positive way sets the tone of the whole comment. It puts the speaker into a positive frame of mind and this is conveyed to the recipient.

Just a little word – **but** what an impact!!

The Invisible 'But'

Here's how the word 'but' can be powerful, even when it's not spoken!

Suppose your child has come home really chuffed because they got eight out of ten in a test. How tempted are you to say, *"Well done (invisible 'but') which ones did you get wrong?"*

Perhaps an older son or daughter achieves six 'A' grades and two 'B's. How many of us are guilty of immediately asking, *"(invisible 'but') Which ones did you get B for?"*

There is an invisible 'but' there, however its presence is every bit as strong.

Tempting though it may be, it is so important not to immediately home straight in on the areas that are less than perfect. Don't diminish their glory – you will be able to find out what you want to know at a later time.

Also, when the time comes, don't criticise all the points that need improving at once. Deal with the major issues first, the minor ones can be dealt with at a later date.

To summarise: Be careful what you say... and watch your but!

Chapter 10

Positive Reinforcement

Indirect Praise
Controlling Your Emotions
What Do You Expect of Your Child?
Beware of Cut-Price Labels!
James' Story
Ignorance is Bliss!
Knowing and Not Knowing
Building on Strengths
Target Your Praise
Daniel's Story
Looking For Opportunities
Nothing Succeeds Like Success
The Feedback Sandwich

Indirect Praise

In Chapter 9 I talked about the damage caused to a child's self-esteem when they overhear you talking about them to another person in a negative manner. However when you become more aware of what you are saying you can use this 'third person' technique in a positive way to create quite the opposite effect and actually boost your child's self-image. In their book, *'How to Talk So Kids Will Listen and Listen So Kids Will Talk'*, Faber and Mazlish emphasise the importance of singing the praises of your child to another adult within the child's hearing.

You can magnify the impact of your praise tenfold through leveraging the third person and this will work wonders for your child's self-esteem.

Try it. Casually say something positive about him to another adult when you are within his earshot and just watch his self-esteem SOAR!

And, in this situation, it doesn't have to be a long detailed account.

A short, *"He was so helpful to me this morning"*

or, *"He's worked so hard today",*

will be just as effective.

 A word of warning here – be genuine. Be careful not to slip into 'Dramatic Mode'. Speaking slowly and loudly and 'putting on' a voice especially for the benefit of your child's listening ears will smack of insincerity.

Just be your normal self. Speak just loud enough for them to hear you and address the adult fully without having one eye on the child. In fact if you can resist glancing at the child at all – looking at the adult instead, your words will have even more impact.

When giving praise in general, make sure you mean what you say. Children quickly see through superficial praise. They need to be able to trust your words and know that you will never say something you don't mean.

Controlling Your Emotions

 Praise which is loaded with emotion can also bring about other unintended results. Children are very perceptive. From a surprisingly young age they can pick up on emotional praise and have their own interpretation of it.

We can all recognise the damage which can be done to a child's self-confidence by us showing an excess of disappointment in their 'failures' but what about showing excess pleasure in their 'successes'? Surely that's a good thing... or is it?

Here lies an important message: When you demonstrate too much elation over a result you are sending various subliminal messages to your child:

Subliminal Message #1 *"It is very important to me that you do well"*

This message implies that if 'doing well' has such a positive emotional effect on you, then it must mean that 'not doing well' will have an equal and opposite negative effect on your emotions. When they don't perform so well they will then feel guilty, and since children, like all of us, are not able to be perfect, this is a huge burden for any child to carry.

Subliminal Message #2 *"I love you only if you do well"*

When you over emphasise your praise, you can give the impression that your love is conditional – yet another reason for not exaggerating when praising your children.

Think about it. If you go completely over the top when your child gets an A Grade and your praise is loaded with emotion, how are they then going to feel when they later have to tell you they got a C? Herein danger lies. You are implying that it means a huge amount to you personally and that you love them for what they achieve not for who they are.

Children then feel they have to always be perfect to gain your love and approval. Your love is seen by them as conditional. They are in danger of growing up into someone who 'beats themselves up' if they're not being perfect at everything they do, which of course is an impossible standard to achieve and can lead to all sorts of problems. This implication of conditional love is another blow for their self-esteem.

Subliminal Message #3 *"I'm surprised – I didn't believe you could do it!"*

This one is a blatant demonstration of your lack of belief in your child – another reason for keeping your emotions on an even keel.

So, all in all, a triple whammy to his self-esteem!

Yet another undesirable effect of over-emotional praise is that it can be used by the child for manipulation. Some children will use bad behaviour to get their own way because you have demonstrated how overly important it is to you that they be good.

In short – praise which is sincere and not overdone is the best praise of all.

What Do You Expect Of Your Child?

⚠ **Children want to please and they will tend to try to live up to your expectations of them. However, whilst the right kind of expectation from parents can be very powerful, the wrong kind of expectation can cause untold damage.**

Let me explain what I mean here:

We have to be aware of the difference between reasonable expectation and unreasonable expectation. It is possible to have expectations which are too high. These are what we call unreasonable expectations and unreasonable expectations create pressure.

Parents who expect their children to have a standard completely beyond their years or to have perfect behaviour, for example, will always be disappointed. The resulting burden of pressure on the child will cause a blow to her self-esteem every time she fails to live up to this impossible standard.

Children should be allowed to be children. Parents should reassure them that it's OK to make mistakes and that no one is perfect – in fact you can demonstrate this by admitting your own mistakes when the opportunity arises and talking about how you can learn from them.

Believing in your child's ability to do something will encourage her own self-belief but having expectations of results which are not fully within her control, or are beyond the capability of a child of her age, means that you risk her falling short of those expectations. Putting children under pressure in this way can cause them to become stressed which could cause damage to their self-confidence for the rest of their lives.

Here's an example: Ground rules – like being polite and saying 'Please' and 'Thank You' and 'Excuse me'; being in bed by a certain time each night; showing respect; telling the truth and so on – are perfectly reasonable expectations because they are actions which are well within the capability of most children. However, always achieving 10 out of 10 in tests, achieving a grade A in his weakest subject, or saving every goal-kick in a game of football, are expectations which are not totally within his control, and are therefore unreasonable expectations.

The true value of expectation is to demonstrate your belief in your child's intention. Expectation then, should not be that he will reach some imposed level of achievement but rather that he will do the best he can do based on his own belief and expectation of himself.

When he does do well you should of course praise him but, at the same time, showing that you are not surprised at his success will show him the strength of your belief in him. After all, when you expect something to happen you are not surprised when it happens and this demonstrates to your child the level of confidence you have in him.

 The key is to remember to praise your child for trying and not to pass judgement or show excessive disappointment or delight in her results.

So having talked about the danger of over-expecting I'm going next to deal with under-expecting.

Beware of Cut-Price Labels!

Expecting your child to throw a wobbly when you ask him to get his coat on because he played up the last time you asked him; expecting him to have poor SATs results because he didn't do so well last time; expecting him to be excessively worried when he visits the dentist, goes on a school trip or has a part in the school play, simply because of past performance, is giving him a label.

And here's the thing: If you do give them a 'cut-price label', you can be sure that children will absolutely live up to that expectation!

⚠ *Giving your child a negative, low-value behaviour or performance-label because of past performance can seriously damage his self-image!*

It is so easy, not just for adults but for children too, to label others by their past behaviour. In one of my classes there were two boys who were both called James and the rest of the class differentiated between the two by calling one 'James' and the other 'Naughty James'! I obviously nipped this in the bud and it didn't continue, but it's an illustration of how easy it is for children to be labelled by their peers.

Another example of this is the child in the classroom situation, who has frequently behaved inappropriately and ends up getting the blame for something he hasn't done.

Once a reputation has been established, whenever an incident happens, other children are quick to blame that young person even if he or she is not guilty: *"Joe spilt that paint"* or *"Sacha took my ruler"*

As adults, **we** need to know better.

The following examples are a perfect illustration of the magic that can happen when we let go of past performance.

James' Story

It is all too easy to judge a child's potential by the performance they have shown to date. Too many children are labelled as 'low ability' and in terms of achieving great things they are, in effect, 'written off'.

I remember well a little boy in my class who was frequently removed from the classroom to get one-to-one help from another adult. In spite of this he showed little progress and, worst of all, he seemed totally disinterested in everything he did. He was becoming more and more introverted and eventually his progress seemed to come to a standstill. It was as if his light was going out.

I negotiated a change in approach and we included him with the rest of the class for a trial period of time. My belief in his ability to cope paid off big time!

The change in attitude was amazing! His sullen expression changed to a look of enthusiasm and sparkle and he positively blossomed!

This new regime was sending a silent message to him which said, *"We believe you can cope"*.

This was just what this particular child needed and his own self-belief and self-image SOARED!

As a result, he applied himself to his work with a diligence and determination we didn't know he had and his all round academic standard visibly improved! He became 'a bright spark'!

Some children undoubtedly benefit from a one-to-one situation for certain things, but for this little boy it was clearly important for him to feel 'one of the gang' and showing him we believed in him rekindled his belief in himself and seemed to make him determined to live up to that image.

To sum up: The following is a simple but profound statement of truth:

 To help your child to build self-belief you absolutely must demonstrate your own, genuine, unwavering belief in your child.

Show your children that you believe in them and they will begin to believe in themselves. . . and their self-confidence will soar!

Here's another story:

Ignorance is Bliss!

"At times our own light goes out and is rekindled by a spark from another person. Each of us has cause to think with deep gratitude of those who have lighted the flame within us."

Albert Schweitzer

In an experiment by Rosenthal and Jacobson[3] all the children in an elementary school were tested and then 20 percent of the pupils were randomly selected regardless of their intellectual competence. The teachers were told that these children had "unusual potential for intellectual growth" and could be expected to make great strides in their academic progress.

After eight months all the children were re-tested. The results were quite remarkable: Every one of those 20 percent who had been labelled 'intelligent' showed a significant improvement in their test results!

The level of results achieved by the children in this experiment had been purely and simply a reflection of the belief and expectation of the teachers!

This experiment focused on positive beliefs and expectations and their influence on academic performance. However, it is reasonable to assume that, had the teachers been told that the children were low achievers, the lower expectations both of the teachers and the children themselves would have resulted in a corresponding decrease in performance.

---

[3] Rosenthal, Robert & Jacobson, Lenore "Pygmalion in the classroom" (1992). Expanded edition. New York: Irvington

Knowing and Not Knowing

In the above experiment, the teachers believed wholeheartedly in the children because they had no reason not to. The strength of their belief led them to expect great results. At this point you may be thinking, "But what about the parent or carer? The belief and expectation they have of their child's ability is influenced by the fact that they *know* what their child is capable of, they *know* their limitations, they know their child inside out"... or do they?

I believe that the average parent is totally unaware of just what their child is capable of achieving when they are given the gift of self-belief – and I'm also including here children with 'special educational needs'.

I'm going to ask you to let go of judgement based on past performance and become fully aware of your own and your child's enormous potential. If there is one thing you need to take on board to succeed it's this:

 Whatever your child has achieved up until this moment in time, is past history. It has absolutely no bearing on what they are capable of achieving from this moment on!

I challenge you to work from this premise!

When you do, you will open up a whole new world of possibilities and you will be amazed at the results.

Whilst the above examples are about believing in a child's academic ability, belief also works like magic with the social, emotional and physical aspects of his life.

In his famous book *'Think and Grow Rich'*, Napoleon Hill tells the remarkable story of his belief in his own son who was born without any ears.

Doctors had told him that the child would be a deaf mute for the rest of his life – but Hill wouldn't accept this. Through his own strong belief and expectation, over the years he planted self-belief and a strong desire in the young mind of the child and, cutting an amazing story short, not only did the boy grow up able to speak and hear, he also went on to help millions of other deaf people around the world!

So is it possible for you, as a parent, to build that firm belief in your child's innate ability – that expectation of the achievement of their true potential?

ABSOLUTELY it is!

And by the time you finish this book you will be equipped with the tools and the know-how to do just that.

Building on Strengths

Still another confidence booster is praising past strengths.

If they belittle their own abilities, you can help your children to increase their self-belief by getting them to revisit a time when they did something particularly well. How did they feel at that time?

A great personal development maxim is "Develop your strengths, manage your weaknesses" This is also applicable to children. Whilst it is necessary for them to have an all round education they will inevitably be weaker in some areas than others.

Try not to draw attention to this. Instead, focus on their strengths. Praising present strengths and calling on past ones will go a long way towards building life-confidence. When faced with a new situation, recalling past successes helps to give the necessary boost to confidence and self-belief, which is needed to overcome our fears and challenges.

Be specific:

Child: *"I'm worried about the school play"*

Parent: *"I'm sure you must feel nervous but just remember that time you played the wicked witch, you were nervous then but as soon as you got onto the stage you were brilliant.*

Everyone said how good you were!"

Target Your Praise

For maximum effect, praise for both past and present successes should be specific. Target your praise whenever possible. Praise which is switched on and delivered as a sweeping statement is not nearly as powerful as targeted praise.

For example:

Instead of: *"Well done"*

Say: *"Well done for tidying your room – I notice you've put those books away really neatly"*

Instead of: *"That's a nice painting"*

Say: *"I like how you've coloured in that bit, I can see you took great care not to go over the line"*

This is targeted praise. It's high impact praise because it demonstrates the sincerity of the person dishing it out.

On the subject of targeted praise and calling on past strengths here's another story:

Daniel's Story

Adults can make a big impact on the mind-set of children by affirming their positive qualities. I have seen this work wonders as the following story shows.

A little boy called Daniel in my class was sitting with his face in his hands during an art lesson. All the others were well into their paintings but Daniel refused to put brush to paper.

When asked, *"What's the matter?"*, he said, *"I'm rubbish at art!"*

I remember his words so clearly. He was certainly being overly hard on himself.

I said to him, *"Well, actually Daniel, I think you're pretty good because I've seen what you've done before so I know you can do some good stuff"* I then went on to remind him of a particular picture he had drawn in his topic book.

It was as if that was all he needed to hear! A look of pride came over his face and he picked up his brush and proceeded to spend the next hour engrossed in his painting and by the end of the lesson he had produced a picture to be proud of!

This isn't rocket science. It only takes a bit of thought to make a huge impact on a child's self esteem.

Looking For Opportunities

Always be on the look out for opportunities to give praise. A child who has sat struggling to do up a button and finally succeeded, may be ignored by a mother who is rushing to get out of the house to meet an older sibling from school.

A child who passes something to you or picks up something you've dropped can go unnoticed if you are engrossed in a conversation with a friend.

Too often moments like these are lost; lost opportunities to add another little brick to the wall of life-confidence. The message is:

 'Catch' them doing well!

Sometimes you miss these opportunities at your peril. For example: When you are preoccupied with a new baby or toddler, an older child may seek your attention in a variety of ways. A young baby can be very demanding and it is easy to let good behaviour go unnoticed. The child who receives very little praise will resort to bad behaviour in order to get attention.

So be on the look out for opportunities to praise and you will stave off the grief of having to deal with jealous aggressive behaviour in the future.

As the song goes 'accentuate the positive – eliminate the negative.' Look out for thoughtful little actions. 'Catch' them doing something right. And if you are too preoccupied at the time, make a mental note to remind them and praise them later, to let them see it didn't go unnoticed.

Here are a few examples:

- You spill some water whilst you are changing a nappy and your older child quickly fetches a cloth for you.

- Your toddler is having a tantrum in the middle of the super-market and your older child helps to put items into the trolley.

- You are feeding your baby and the phone rings. Your older child immediately brings it to you.

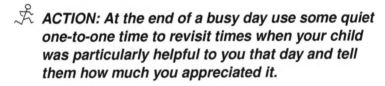 *ACTION: At the end of a busy day use some quiet one-to-one time to revisit times when your child was particularly helpful to you that day and tell them how much you appreciated it.*

There are a myriad of opportunities to give targeted praise. Don't miss them!

Nothing Succeeds Like Success

"Nothing succeeds like success"

Alexandre Dumas

Experience has shown that it takes many more items of praise to balance one item of criticism. It's a fact that the human mind tends to recall the negative experiences in life more vividly than the positive ones. It seems that negative experiences leave a much longer lasting impression on our psyche than positive ones. When we think back to childhood the negative incidents always stick in our minds. (A big one for me was arriving at school at five years old and realising I had forgotten to put my knickers on! I was devastated and I have never forgotten it.)

We humans have a natural instinct to notice the negative stuff and to home in on failures. Where your child is concerned, it's important that you resist this at all costs. Focus your attention on what he has achieved, however small.

Things like: Finishing the cross country race; singing in the choir; raising £10 at the school fair; improving his marks in a maths test; passing her cycling proficiency test; getting homework done without having to be reminded. This will boost them to build on their successes and achieve even more.

Believe it or not children are fully in tune with their weaknesses and don't need us to point them out and make them feel even more worthless!

The Feedback Sandwich

There will of course be occasions when it is appropriate, and indeed helpful, to discuss ways in which your child could improve, but this should be done in a positive, constructive way.

The word criticism implies judgement. I prefer to call it constructive feedback.

One of the most positive ways to give feedback is to sandwich just one or two suggestions between praise. Begin with some targeted praise, then offer suggestions as to how improvements could be made in future, then follow with more praise.

Here's an example of a 'Feedback Sandwich':

"I can see you've made a real effort to tidy your bedroom Gabbie, those books look really neat."

"Perhaps you could make the boxes a bit safer by starting with the biggest ones then put the medium sized ones on top and the small ones last."

"That carpet looks lovely and clear now though. Well done!"

An even better approach would be to present the above constructive feedback (the middle of the sandwich) in the form of a question rather than a suggestion (i.e be non-directive):

"Those boxes look a bit unsafe. What could you do to make sure they don't fall over?"

or, *"How could you make those boxes a bit safer?"*

When we have a healthy dose of praise (the 'bread' in the sandwich) our confidence is boosted and we are much more able to take some constructive criticism (the 'filling').

The message is: The best way to help your child to grow in confidence is to home in on the things he is doing well.

Chapter 11

Who's in Charge?

How Would Your Child Cope Without You?

Have you ever wondered how your child/children would cope if you were suddenly taken seriously ill? Not a very nice thought I know, but you will do them a great favour if you allow yourself to think it.

Whether or not the unthinkable should happen, it is your job as a parent to make your children independent. For some parents that's a tough one as parents have needs of their own and may not want to let their child go (especially if it's their youngest), after all – those parents will then eventually have to come to terms with not being needed!

But guess what...

 Your job is to help your children not to need you!

If you are needy they will be needy too! And neediness and self-confidence do not go together. Holding on to our children for as long as we can is selfish because we are not doing them any favours, merely making them dependent.

If the concept of letting them go feels uncomfortable to you, you may need to do a bit of work on your own issues around self-confidence and neediness and take an honest look at whose best interest you are serving.

It is the responsibility of parents to allow their children enough space to be developing human beings within a framework. Lessons learnt from our own mistakes are lessons never forgotten.

Encouraging independence from an early age is very important in building life-confidence. Take getting dressed: Tying shoe laces; doing up zips and buttons; turning jumpers the right way – these are all things a three year old should be practising on a daily basis with your constant background encouragement.

Of course it's always quicker if you do these things for them, and sometimes you have to. However, in the rush of everyday life it's very easy to overlook the importance of allowing time for your child to practise these skills. She will be expected to do these basic tasks herself when she is at school and it can cause unnecessary stress for her if she is not capable doing them.

Not building time in the day for these things will mean your children are unprepared for school life. If they see other children coping on their own when they themselves are struggling, their self-confidence will take a knock.

In addition, from a teacher's point of view, time spent waiting for a class to get dressed and undressed for PE will encroach on valuable lesson time.

Other things such as tidying away toys, helping to lay the table and so on, all encourage independence and independence helps with self-confidence. A child of eight for example is quite capable of using the washing machine and getting their own breakfast whilst a four year old can tidy their toys and carry their plate to the sink.

Encouraging these helpful gestures also helps them to consider your feelings.

The message here is this:

 When you encourage them to do things for themselves from a young age you are actually putting your children's needs before your own.

Taking responsibility for their own actions builds their life-confidence.

Teaching your children to become independent does not mean you love them less. We can express our love for our children in many different ways without the need to be their servant.

Being a loving parent means spending quality time with them, listening to their problems, being understanding, respecting their feelings, doing fun things together, loving them unconditionally, and all the time – making sure they are equipped with oodles of life-confidence as a result of developing their independence.

When the time comes to let your children go, your task will be made much easier if you have equipped them with an abundance of independence and life-confidence. In addition, you will have brought your children up to be respectful of other people's feelings and to take responsibility for themselves.

Are You Over Protecting?

As they get older, we need to be aware of that fine line between keeping our children safe from serious harm, and allowing them to learn for themselves. Most parents don't have to work at being protective, it's a natural instinct. What we do need to guard against however, is being over-protective.

 It is so easy to become over-protective, and over-protected children can grow up to be people who are lacking in life-confidence and afraid to take any risks.

Now I don't suppose you know many parents who wave their children good bye and say *"Bye darling. Make sure you take lots of risks today!"* But a lot of parents are at the opposite end of the spectrum and send out the message that the world is a very dangerous place to be.

My father's words always ring in my ears to this day, *"Keep your wits about you"* he would say frequently, meaning *"It's a bad world out there and you need to keep looking over your shoulder for danger"*. Of course we want our children to be aware of dangers but we also need to keep things in proportion.

I still struggle not to say those very same words too often to my own children, even though they are now adults, soon to have children of their own!

The fact is, as well as 'keeping their wits about them', children need to be allowed to take some risks. They need to risk making mistakes whilst at the same time being protected against serious harm. It's a matter of getting the balance right.

Parents who over-protect have the mistaken belief that their children are incapable of coping with even the most basic of activities and the more children are over-protected, the more needy they become until the whole scenario becomes a self-fulfilling prophesy.

I grew up as the youngest of three, my sisters being a good many years older than me. Ours was a close knit family with my aunt and my grandmother living in with us. Being the 'baby' of the family I had plenty of people who felt I needed protecting and it was a long time before I took on any responsibility.

This of course was to have a knock-on effect on my confidence.

What's interesting is, looking back through my life, on my journey towards adulthood I gravitated towards people with dominating personalities. People who put me down in order to boost themselves. My lack of confidence became a self-fulfilling prophesy!

Over-protected, or over-parented children become dependent upon the guidance and advice of others; are unable to make decisions of their own without seeking the approval of others; are afraid to take risks; are generally lacking in life-confidence. It is of paramount importance for parents to get the balance right between protecting children from harm and allowing them to take risks and learn from their own mistakes.

Assessing Risk

Some activities are obviously riskier than others, but the trick is to weigh up the risks of your children being harmed. If you practise assessing the chances of a negative result and the impact of that result, it is possible to protect them from serious harm whilst still encouraging them to take smaller risks.

 ACTION: Look for opportunities to talk through the possible outcomes of an activity with your child to help her to develop the skill of assessing and minimising risk herself.

Here's an example:

"If you carry all those heavy boxes at once what might happen?"

"What's the best way of carrying them so they won't fall on your toes?"

Children are capable of doing more than we realise and the more we encourage them to do for themselves, the bigger the favour we are doing them.

Keeping a Watchful Eye

Parents quite rightly keep a watchful eye on wandering toddlers for fear they may run away.

I remember watching an interesting study produced for UK television many years ago. It showed a mother sitting outdoors with her 2 year old toddler.

The mother had been instructed that at no time should she call out to her child, in fact she was to give the appearance of not even watching him. They were filmed over a period of time and the film was then speeded up.

The findings were fascinating. It was as if the toddler was connected to the mother by an invisible cord, as if there was an invisible force-field around the mother keeping him within a set radius.

The child would go a certain distance away and then turn around and come running back.

The amazing thing was whichever direction he went, the distance from the mother was the same – and not once did the mother call out to him! Even at such a young age, this toddler had a certain awareness of taking responsibility for his safety!

Now I'm not advocating for one moment that parents should be any less vigilant with their children. On the contrary there are many dangers which they need protecting from, according to the situation, which they may not be old enough to understand.

What I am saying is, when in a safe environment it's a good idea to practise being more discreet with our vigilance, i.e. keep a watchful eye but don't let your child see you are watching him. This encourages him to keep an eye on you thus developing his own awareness and responsibility from an early age.

ROLE MODEL: What about your own confidence? Do you always play it safe or are you a risk taker? How confident are you in your child's eyes?

As with decision making which I shall cover shortly, the way you approach unfamiliar tasks and sum up the risks involved, will be closely monitored by your children. If they perceive you to be lacking in confidence by both your words and actions, their own confidence may be affected.

Your child may worry and even feel responsible if they see you worrying and fearful. Remember, whenever they are in earshot and eyeshot they will be looking to you for their role model. Your attitude to life will be mirrored by your children so keep working on yourself!

Terrible Tantrums

The first signs of a child asserting their independence and wanting to take control of their own actions, are the 'terrible tantrums' or 'the terrible twos' as they are often called. And don't they always happen in the most public of places!

I once came across a little girl having a tantrum when I was doing my weekly Sainsbury's shop. Her screams I'm sure could be heard from out on the street. As I turned into the aisle there was the toddler with her father. She was red in the face, stamping and yelling and everyone in the shop was staring at this poor man! I felt sorry for him but he seemed totally unaffected by the whole incident. He simply went about filling his trolly as if his daughter wasn't there and every now and then he would talk to her in a very calm matter-of-fact voice making it clear that he was not going to be drawn in to giving attention to such behaviour. Eventually his calm attitude paid off. The child stopped screaming and the tantrum came to an end. I was so impressed with how he had dealt with the situation I went up to the gentleman in question and told him so. "Ah" he said with a smile, "I'm used to it!"

Tantrums are a part of growing up, and whilst it's sometimes possible to divert your child's attention to avoid confrontation, very often the only way out of them is 'through' them! Children should not be allowed to use them to manipulate you into giving in to them. (You can find more tips on dealing with tantrums in my ebook "From Tantrum Tots to Teenage Strops").

Choices

As they get older, children begin to assert their independence even more and can still display moments of stubbornness. On these occasions, winning the battle of wills often becomes more important to them than avoiding doing what they were asked to do in the first place!

Giving your child choices whenever possible can help to avoid a potential confrontation and it's also a way of encouraging their independence, building the foundations for giving them a certain amount of ownership of their life.

When you find yourself in a 'stale mate' situation where your child is stubbornly refusing to do as you ask, choices can often come to the rescue.

I can best illustrate this with another story:

Jennie's Story

My first introduction to Jennie was hearing her screams and sobs from the other end of the corridor. I was doing a day's supply teaching in a school I hadn't taught in before and it was play time. Jennie, who was 5 years old, had not made it to the toilet in time and her knickers were soaking wet.

I went to see what the screams were about and found the little girl in a very distressed state, surrounded by two lunchtime supervisors and the school secretary. They were all trying to persuade her to change her knickers and she was refusing, point blank, to co-operate.

The three adults had tried patiently to reason with Jennie, saying things like, *"You'll get a sore bottom"* and *"Mummy won't be very pleased if you have wet pants"* but she was having none of it.

I asked them to let me have a quiet word with her. I took her to one side and, knowing that all reasoning had failed, I said,

"Jennie. You can't stay in wet knickers all the afternoon. When would you like to change them? Playtime's nearly finished. You can either change them now and get it done or you can wait 'till playtime's over and do it then. When would you like to do it?"

The little girl stopped crying in an instant, and she simply said, *"Now"*!

Why had this worked so well? Going from everyone telling her she had to do something, to being given the responsibility for choosing what she did, gave her back her power. It put her back in control and instantly transformed her attitude.

By being given a choice the confrontation situation was broken, and she was able to accept the fact that, whether she changed her knickers or not was simply not negotiable! She still emerged having retained some control over the situation. I suspect that the thought of the other children coming in and seeing her having to change her knickers could have had something to do with the decision to act! Nevertheless that decision was hers.

Handing over responsibility to your children by giving them the opportunity to make their own choices, is a powerful way to build their life-confidence. Children can learn to make simple choices from a very young age, sowing the seeds of independence and self-reliance.

Allowing your child to choose is not only very empowering for her but it can also get you out of some tricky confrontational situations as the story above illustrates.

Just think about this for a moment. If you were constantly being told what to do and expected to obey without question, and often without explanation, how would you feel? I know how I'd feel! I would feel controlled, indignant, powerless, resentful and angry! Children feel like this too.

Some children find it difficult to make choices if given more than a couple of options, especially if they have not been accustomed to choosing. Keeping to the 'either or' choice will help them here, and this also allows you to have some control in the matter, whilst at the same time giving them some responsibility.

Start to give your children choices in their early years. Choices like which vegetables to eat; which shoes to wear; which story to have; whether to clear away the bricks first or the Lego; whether to hold on to your hand or the buggy – the list is endless.

These are seemingly insignificant things, but together they help children to feel in control of their lives and therefore develop their confidence. They also help to keep stress and conflict to a minimum.

Preparation Time

Children don't like commands and orders suddenly sprung on them. Who does? It does nothing for their independence, takes away their power and often causes resistance. The sudden announcement of "Bedtime!" for example, when they are in the middle of a computer game is just asking for conflict.

When there is something you need your children to do, if you give them some preparation time first you are far more likely to enlist their cooperation.

Using the bedtime scenario as an example, try giving a countdown:

"It's bedtime at 8 o'clock so don't get too many toys out now"

then: *"Ten minutes to go so we need to start clearing the floor"*

and: *"Five more minutes to go then you need to come and clean your teeth"*

If you find yourself in a conflict situation it is sometimes helpful to give choices around something not directly related to the desired outcome. For example, if the final announcement of "Bedtime!" instigates tears and potentially the start of a battle, all is not lost. Try deflecting attention from bedtime for the moment and offer a distraction in the form of a choice:

e.g. *"We've got to get these toys cleared away, what are you going to clear first, the puzzle or the pens?"*

This can diffuse the situation and restore harmony.

Three words about bedtime: Make it pleasurable!

Making bedtime something to look forward to can avoid untold battles. One way to do this is to use it for some quality time. A story, a cuddle, a chat about pleasurable things, all help to make going to bed something to look forward to and at the same time will put your child into a relaxed state. This is also a good time to do a guided visualisation (see Chapters 12 and 14).

Making Decisions – It's No Big Deal!

Decision making is an important skill to teach your children. We have already talked about giving children the opportunity to choose and even restricted choices are a good introduction to the skill of decision making.

ROLE MODEL: Here, as with all other areas, it is important to be a good role model for your children. If they see you being decisive they will pick up on the message that decision making is no big deal. A lot of time and energy can be wasted by being indecisive and hovering between one decision and another and indecisiveness indicates a lack of confidence.

Whatever situation you find yourself in there will be pros and cons, but if you have trained yourself to make the best of things, making decisions will not be such a problem. The main thing is not to waste too much time deciding. It is better to make a poor decision than not to make any decision at all. No decision = no progress.

Confident people are decisive people.

All of the most successful people in this world are quick to make decisions and slow to change their minds.

In other words, whatever you decide, you can make it work. If things don't work out immediately it's not a problem – you simply make another decision.

This decisive strategy reminds me of my husband when we're out driving and he takes the wrong road. Instead of stopping, pondering, dithering or turning back he calmly continues going forward, without fussing, and takes another route.

If that one isn't quite getting us to where we want to be he confidently and decisively takes another, and another until we arrive at our destination.

Now he may be saving face and not wanting to admit he's gone wrong by turning back! However, I'm giving him the benefit of the doubt and saying he's decisive and forward thinking!

Collaboration versus Direction

As they get older you can encourage your children to progress to more considered decisions by asking the right kind of questions. The essence of good coaching and good teaching alike, is to facilitate the student to think things through for themselves by asking open ended questions.

Parenting is no exception. Get into the habit of taking every opportunity to get your children thinking for themselves.

Beginning questions with the word 'What' or the word 'How' is a good rule to remember.

Instead of *"Why don't you write a note to remind yourself to do your homework?*

Try saying *"What could you do to make sure you remember your homework?"*

Instead of, *"Why don't you set the alarm clock so you're not late for rehearsals?"*

Try saying, *"How can you make sure you are on time for rehearsals?"*

or *"What needs to happen for you to be on time for rehearsals?"*

Children will often come up with good ideas that you hadn't even thought of!

Other words to begin open-ended, solution-oriented questions are 'Who', 'When' and 'Where':

"Who could you ask to help you solve that problem?"

"When would be a good time to get your homework done?"

"Where could you look for that information?"

Be careful of using the word 'Why' as this can come over as being judgemental.

This non-directive or collaborative approach is far more effective in that it encourages analytical thinking and gives the child ownership of the course of action. Actions which children have come up with themselves stand a far better chance of being carried out, and when you empower them to solve their own problems you are placing another brick in that wall of life-confidence.

As a teacher, children are constantly asking me questions, and with 30+ children to deal with it would be so easy and so quick just to give them the answers. For the teacher and parent alike however, this is false economy of time.

When you involve your child in the solution to the problem, you are helping them to develop independence and this will save you more time in the long run. You are also encouraging them to make their own decisions.

Example:

Child: *"Where shall I put this paper?"*

Option 1 – Directive answer making the child more dependent:

Adult *"Over on that table"*

Option 2 – Collaborative answer encouraging independence:

Adult *"Where do you think would be a good place to put it?"*

If the child still doesn't know, you can give them a choice of two or more places. Children should be taught that there are no wrong or right decisions, just choices.

In a class of children it is always easy to spot those who have not been encouraged to think for themselves and therefore lack confidence. They will be the ones who ask questions which have the most obvious of answers. I always turn the question around and ask it back. If they are still unsure I say, *"What do you think I might say?"* and they nearly always come up with a sensible answer.

When you take this approach it's imperative that you allow enough thinking time for your child. We have all been guilty of not giving children sufficient time to think things through when we ask them a question, and it's important to make a concerted effort to allow for silence.

When I ask a class, *"Do you think grown-ups give you lots of time or not enough time to think of the answers?"* – as I have done many times – a minimum of 75% always say they'd like more time.

Try the 9 second rule: When you ask a question count up to 9 slowly in your head before speaking again. It may seem an age to you but it's a fleeting moment for the person thinking of the answer.

So the message of The First Pillar of Life-Confidence can be summed up in one sentence – namely: A strong self-belief is a prerequisite, both for your own success as a parent and a person, and for your child's success too.

Now for The Second Pillar of Life-Confidence:

As well as truly believing in your potential, the next ingredient of The B.E.S.T. Success Formula is also crucial to achieving life-success.

That ingredient is ENTHUSIASM!

PART 3

The Second Pillar of

Life-Confidence:

nthusiasm

"Enthusiasm is that secret and harmonious spirit
which hovers over the production of genius"
Isaac Disraeli

Chapter 12

Building Your Dream

"Yeah But..."
Strategies to Beat the Dream Stealers
Setting Goals
Aligning Your Main Goal With Your Values and Passions
Making Your Main Goal Big
Making Your Main Goal Clear
Visualisation
The Greatest DVD
Affirmations
Expectation
Attitude

The Dream Stealers

"Watch out! Watch out!
The Dream Stealers are about!
They're after your hopes and your dreams.
And all through the day,
They're working away,
And nothing is quite what it seems.
They come in disguise.
There's belief in their eyes.
Their words have you fooled through and through.
Their intentions are kind,
But their thoughts make them blind,
'Cos they've had their dreams stolen too!"

Sue Atkinson

Usually children are wonderfully uninhibited and have big dreams but as they grow up those dreams are sabotaged by... 'The Dream Stealers'.

'The Dream Stealers' are the people children interact with in every-day life: people with limiting beliefs who have had their own dreams stolen many years ago when they were children – stolen by people who had their dreams stolen... by people who had their dreams stolen... back and back in time!

And here's the key...

 Our biggest dream-stealers are often those people who are closest to us – our own family!

"Yeah But..."

Do those two words sound familiar? When you hear them – duck; start whistling; walk away! go to the loo; go and feed the chickens; sing to the cat; anything! Just don't allow them to penetrate your sub-conscious mind.

See if you recognise any of the following examples:

  "Yeah but don't be daft, you'll never be able to do that"

  "Yeah but you're no good at talking to people"

  "Yeah but you can't afford it"

  "Yeah but you're not qualified"

  "Yeah but you don't have the time"

And here's a good one...

  "Yeah but you've got to be realistic!"

The list goes on.

Dream Stealers don't do it knowingly. They do it because they are not familiar with thinking big dreams and it doesn't sit comfortably with them. They do it because they are afraid they might lose you if you start to think differently. They do it because they've had *their* dreams stolen.

The saddest thing about The Dream Stealers is that when we allow them to influence our thoughts, we begin to sabotage our own aspirations – we become the stealer of our own dreams!

Always remember this:

 You have a power within you which is far greater than any challenge you may come across in your lifetime and, make no mistake about it, that power is awesome!

You are capable of great things, but your childhood dreams and aspirations were most probably quelled long ago. So here's the question...

 Do you want to be the one to steal your children's dreams?

Do you want to be the one who makes them settle for second best for the rest of their lives? Of course you don't. This brings us back to why it is so important that you develop yourself alongside your children.

Without doubt you are the biggest cog in the wheel of your child's life.

I'm going to give you some strategies to beat The Dream Stealers but before I do, I want to remind you how powerful your mind is and what a vast amount of untapped potential you have in reserve. To illustrate this let's look at an analogy:

Flick That Switch!

Imagine for a moment you are standing in a vast stadium and it is pitch dark. Now imagine that the only light you can see in that black void comes from one tiny, birthday-cake candle which you are holding in your hand. What you don't realise is that on the wall in the darkness is a light-switch capable of flooding the whole stadium with the brightest light.

The ratio of that minute area of candle-light to the infinite darkness around you can be compared to the portion of the mind which the average person uses compared to their whole potential!

Staying with this analogy: A fit, healthy, active young child is born with a huge amount of enthusiasm for life and has a 'light' inside them (their potential) which, if we find the 'switch', is equivalent to illuminating ten stadiums – achieving magnificent life-success and life-confidence!

It is your job to make sure your child's enthusiasm is not restricted and his light dimmed as he grows older, but channelled and directed like a search-light so that his full potential can be reached. And that potential is just awesome!

So when are you going to flick that switch?

When we think of something we'd love to do, our old negative conditioning rears its ugly head and immediately that voice in our head thinks of all the reasons why we can't do it – and of course The Dream Stealers will always be there to agree.

However, this book is about all the reasons why you *can* do it!

Strategies to Beat the Dream Stealers

"Tread softly, for you tread on my dreams"

William Blake

Setting Goals

In his famous best seller *"Think and Grow Rich"*, Napoleon Hill writes of a secret formula for success, common to the world's most successful people. This secret formula is to set yourself a goal and commit it to paper.

Studies of the world's most successful people have revealed that one factor they have in common is that they all have very clear goals, and they all write them down.

Knowing what you want (your main, long-term, 'dream' goal) and making a plan as to how you are going to go about getting it (your medium to short term 'journey' goals) gives you a head start.

Confident people set goals.

The importance of setting yourself a goal and then putting in a plan of action to move you towards that goal cannot be overemphasised. It will give you a definite purpose for living and it will ensure that you are constantly growing and expanding.

I shall talk about the 'journey goals' – your 'Targeted Action Steps' – in Section 5. For now I want to concentrate on the importance of building your enthusiasm for your main dream goal – whatever that might be.

If we have no set goals in life we are drifting, and if we are drifting we are following somebody else's goals. Goals are all about taking control of your own life and setting yourself firmly in the driving seat.

Of course when you are in the driving seat of your own life you are in the very best position to help your children to drive their lives.

Whilst motivation is an external stimulus, enthusiasm is an internal state of being – it comes from a state of inspiration.

Enthusiasm is a necessary emotional state to get you into action and also to help you to maintain that action when things don't go according to plan. Enthusiasm is critical and will undoubtedly be a huge boost to your confidence.

To build unshakeable enthusiasm about doing something, in addition to believing in yourself, you need something else. That something is a burning desire to achieve. In other words a passion.

Napoleon Hill devotes a whole chapter to Desire in his book *'Think and Grow Rich'*. For the purpose of this book I've added an addendum to that famous quote:

> *"Anything you can conceive and believe, you can achieve"*
> *... providing your desire is strong enough*

So how do you go about building that strong desire – that passion?

Firstly, making time to contemplate what you truly want and why you want it is imperative to your success. In order to build that desire within you and beat the dream stealers you need to be inspired from within, and to get inspired you need to have a goal which excites you – a really big dream. At the same time you need to develop your imagination.

Your main dream goal must have the following attributes:

- It must be aligned with your values and passions
- It must be big
- It must be clear

I'd like to talk about each of those three things in turn:

Aligning Your Main Goal With Your Values And Passions

As I have already stressed you must become emotionally involved with your goals, and to do that you need to have ownership of them. By that I mean, they need to be your own goals and not someone else's – only then will you be truly inspired to achieve them.

Author and speaker Dr John Demartini talks extensively about the importance of values and likens a person's hierarchy of values to fingerprints; I like to think of them as being like snowflakes – unlike any other – and, just as it's impossible to change the pattern of a snowflake, so it is a waste of time trying to change someone's value pattern to fit your own.

To become inspired, a person's goals need to be in line with their own hierarchy of values. In other words a goal must be aligned to something that is truly important to you, just as your child's goals must be aligned to something important to them in order for them to generate sufficient passion.

The main problem most people have is that their goals are set for them by someone else – usually their boss! And children are no exception. They have their goals set by authority figures like their parents, their teachers, their football coach etc.

In schools, although target setting takes place, the goals are largely teacher directed because they are dictated by the requirements of the curriculum. What's more, with a class full of children to get through, teachers can only spend a short time with each child on goal-setting and, due to this time pressure, targets are often set with more input from the teacher than the child and with precious little negotiation.

But the fact is, a goal set by anyone other than the person concerned is totally uninspiring.

 For a goal to stand the best chance of succeeding it must be conceived by the person who the goal is for.

When they are young children learn the basic socialisation values from their parents and other adult role models – values such as telling the truth, respecting the feelings of others, respecting property etc. As they grow up they begin to adopt additional values of their own and their combination of values becomes unique to them.

Time taken to consider what is truly valuable to your children will reap rewards both for them and for you.

It's impossible to go through life completely without having some goals imposed upon us from outside, but even when tasks are set for children by others – for example school work – although it takes some thought, it is still possible to help them to link the goals to their values and passions.

But this process takes time. It involves allowing time to coach them and facilitate them to make choices and to take ownership of their goals, and as I said earlier, time is a commodity which is in short supply for our busy teachers. However it is time which is so well spent!

Trying to get a child to be motivated to do something which reflects your values and not theirs will, at best, produce mediocre results because the child's heart will not be in it; at worse it will be like banging your head against a brick wall.

Always have *their* values in mind. For example, if you want your child to spend more time getting their homework done but playing with their friends is higher on their values list you could point out to them that being good at your school work will make you more popular with your friends.

John Demartini, who talks in depth about the importance of ascertaining your hierarchy of values, tells the story of a mother who came to him at her wits end because her son could not be dragged away from the computer. He played games at every available moment and this was the cause of much conflict because the mother felt he should be spending more time on his studies (this was high on *her* list of values). Here was an obvious conflict of values.

Dr Demartini asked to see the son and after talking to him discovered that he was actually highly skilled on the computer. He told the child's mother what a whiz-kid her son was and advised her to channel his talents.

The mother heeded his words and encouraged her son to use the computer in a more productive way and the boy grew up to be a top computer programmer with a job which commanded a high salary and, what's more, he loved what he did because he was following his passion!

 ACTION: When you are next negotiating with your child, be aware of their values and passions and point out ways in which they would benefit from what you are suggesting. This is an invaluable strategy for maintaining harmony and co-operation.

Making Your Main Goal Big

When setting goals many people underestimate that massive potential they have within them, which I talked about earlier. They therefore play it safe and only set goals which are realistic, down to earth and easily achieved. Consequently their goals are not exciting enough to ignite their enthusiasm and spur them into action.

It's human nature to want to stay within our comfort zone and not stretch ourselves to achieve more. The problem with that is, when we stay too long in our comfort zone we can slip into lethargy, boredom and even depression. In order to grow and move forward we need to stretch ourselves a little beyond the familiar.

Goals which are small and easy to achieve are not as inspiring and exciting as big goals. When setting big goals you don't need to know the 'how', you just need to have a big enough 'why' and the 'how' will take care of itself in the form of your small 'journey goals' which I call 'Targeted Action Steps'.

So don't discourage your child if they come up with what may seem to you to be an 'unrealistic' dream (I shall explore goal setting further in Part 5). Suffice to say: Encourage those big aspirations!

Making Your Main Goal Clear

Most people don't dwell long enough on their dream in order to build their desire i.e. they don't build a clear enough picture of what they want. When you have chosen an appropriate goal, you need to take time to really think about that goal; to imagine how you will feel when you've achieved it and to revisit it on a regular basis – only then will you acquire the persistence needed to hang in there when the going gets tough. A good tool to help you to do this with your child is Visualisation.

Visualisation

Helping children to build a clear image of their desire, building up that desire into a passion and visualising how things will be when they have achieved it, makes so much sense.

 The scope of a young child's imagination is massive! They are far better at it than us! What an opportunity we are missing then if we don't use it!

Visualisation is merely a process of engaging the imagination and all the senses to form a clear vision of the things you want. You can do this by yourself or with another person.

Visualisation is an essential tool to induce positive thinking and to keep those dream stealers at bay. The efficacy of its results has been well documented: Famous sportsmen use visualisation to great effect when they envisage themselves scoring a goal, executing a perfect golf swing or winning a race.

When you talk someone through a visualisation it's known as Guided Visualisation or Guided Imagery, and the person being guided visualises a situation as they want it to be (more about this in Chapter 14). I have had great success using this technique both with children and adults, and it can be used for a variety of purposes.

Guided Visualisation is used in complementary therapy, helping patients to enter a relaxed peaceful state to stimulate their immune response and speed up recovery. This process can be very powerful and has even been used with cancer patients to bring about a state of remission, which, in some cases can be long lasting.

Getting your child to take themselves forward in time and imagine how they will feel when they have achieved their goal is a great way to keep the dream alive.

I wonder how many people remember being told off for daydreaming when they were at school. Children are visualising when they are daydreaming and it can in fact be a good thing to do when the mind is being programmed with positive thoughts. Guided Visualisation is a bit like directing a daydream but to a more intense level.

When talking your children through a visualisation it is important to involve as many of the senses as possible. When the senses are involved a bio-chemical response is set up in the body and you make a more lasting, vivid impression on the sub-conscious mind. The visualisation will be much more powerful as a result. And remember – the sub-conscious mind cannot tell the difference between fiction and reality.

Get them to imagine how they are feeling; build up the scene in detail, seeing the shapes and colours, hearing the sounds and, if applicable, smelling the scents. (Visualisation can also be used to great effect for helping to dissipate stress and worry – see Chapter 14).

The Greatest DVD

In his fascinating book *'Psycho-Cybernetics'* (see also Chapters 4 and 18) Maxwell Maltz talks about making a 'Mental Movie'. When you close your eyes you imagine a giant screen on the wall of your mind and you are watching a DVD with you as the star. You run this through and see yourself as the person you want to be in any given situation. See the people around you smiling in appreciation and take note of the confidence in your expression, your voice and your posture.

Help your child to run his 'Mental Movie' on the screen of his mind on a regular daily basis and his whole attitude will eventually begin to change.

 ACTION: Set aside some uninterrupted time to talk about your child's dreams and aspirations and run their 'Mental Movie'. What would they like to be when they grow up? What would they like to do? What would they really love to have? How will it make them feel when they reach their goal? What will be happening around them? What will they be seeing/hearing? What will others be saying?

Affirmations

Affirmations can be a very powerful way of eliminating limiting beliefs from your child's mind. They are short words or phrases, which are written down and read back daily. Affirmations are statements which you imagine to be true. And 'imagine' is the operative word. This point is crucial: To be effective they must be read with imagination and emotion.

Although schools still have a long way to go, it has to be said that some life-confidence strategies are beginning to seep into the education system – one of which is affirmations. You may have seen positive words or phrases displayed in your child's school – however the bad news is they are generally not used effectively, so what could potentially be a powerful tool is rendered next to useless.

⚠ ***Without emotional involvement, affirmations will fall on deaf ears and blind eyes. Focus is the key.***

Affirmations are useless unless the reader becomes emotionally involved with their message. Many people make the mistake of merely reading out their affirmations in a mechanical fashion. It's a bit like reading a book when your mind is on something else. You can read a whole paragraph only to realise that you haven't taken in one word and have no idea what it's about.

Focus is the key with affirmations. When used in conjunction with visualisations they can be extremely powerful. Ideally they should be written by the child. **Affirmations should be positively stated and written in the present.** For example, to eliminate a limiting belief about a lack of ability in a certain area, say a spelling test,

instead of: *"I'm not going to get any spellings wrong"*

substitute: *"I am getting all my spellings right"*

Regular repetition and visualisation of the affirmations, will eventually lodge the thoughts into the sub-conscious mind and the child will begin to change their whole attitude, until they will begin to act differently, bringing a change in results.

I would love to see schools making more use of affirmations.

A good example of this would be to get the children to write them down on a regular daily basis. They could even fill in their own blank report sheet at the beginning of the year writing it like an affirmation – in the present tense as if it has already happened. What a motivation! What a goal to aspire to!

Other examples of affirmations are:

"I am getting better and better at my reading"

"I am very popular with the rest of the class"

"I have some good friends"

"My football skills are improving every day"

"I have great fun in PE lessons"

Allow your children to make up and write their own, as this will have more meaning for them. If they are too young, you can write for them but make sure you write them in your child's own words. This will make it more personal and be easier for them to read back and is a great communication exercise in itself.

ROLE MODEL: Have your own affirmations posted around the house and let your child see you reading them. Give yourself time to visualise and meditate (see Chapter 14), fifteen minutes is good – half an hour is even better. However, even the odd five minutes will be better than nothing at all, but to have an effect it needs to be done regularly. Plan it into your day. It's helpful to get into the habit of doing it around the same time each day. If this time is when your children are at school, make sure you occasionally let them see you sitting quietly, relaxing with your eyes closed, breathing calmly and perhaps saying your affirmations out loud.

ACTION: Get your child to tell you how he/she would really like things to be if you could wave a magic wand. Then get them to write this down on a piece of card or a gummed label. Put it in a place where they will see it when they first get up in the morning and when they go to bed at night. Encourage them to read it aloud as often as possible and combine this with a guided visualisation to get them imagining how they will feel when they have achieved their dream.

Expectation

Earlier I talked about the expectation we have of our children and how important it is to get the balance right – i.e. showing enough expectation to show you believe in them but making sure your expectations are realistic and you are not putting them under pressure. I call this 'External Expectation'

Now I want to talk about a very different and far more powerful kind of expectation and that is 'Internal Expectation'.

Internal Expectation is the most powerful expectation of all because, as the name implies, it comes from within. Rather than being imposed from outside it is self-generated. And that's what makes it so powerful.

Internal Expectation is the magic that happens when your belief in your ability to achieve your goals becomes so strong it turns into expectation. It's the difference between motivation and inspiration: External Expectation motivates, Internal Expectation inspires.

It is your job to help your child to make his belief system so powerful; his enthusiasm so strong, that it automatically turns into internal expectation.

It's impossible to recognise the point of change. Belief, enthusiasm and expectation are like the colours of a rainbow – there's no demarcation between where one ends and the other begins. The aim is to practise positive thinking and self-belief to such a degree that you cannot help but pass into a state of expectation – you begin to *expect* your desire to materialise.

And once you begin to expect things to happen you bring the law of attraction into action and corresponding results will appear in your life like magic!

Isn't this great stuff?

A great book for further reading on how the law of attraction works is *'You Were Born Rich'* by Bob Proctor.

So what causes your internal expectation to be reflected in the results you get in your life?

It's all about Attitude.

Attitude

Your attitude is the outward reflection of your thoughts and feelings. In other words, the image you portray to the outside world is congruent with what you are thinking and feeling on the inside. If you think positive thoughts you will feel positive feelings and your resulting attitude will be positive too.

Research has shown that a whopping 93% of all communication is attributed to tone of voice, actions and body language[4]. So BEWARE!

 If you think negative thoughts about someone, however hard you try to cover them up with the things you say, your attitude will usually give the game away!

Perhaps the most exciting thing about building enthusiasm and expectation is this: The resulting change in your attitude, has a knock-on effect on the way others behave towards you! It's true that we can only change ourselves – we can't change others – but here's the paradox: The delicious truth is that when we change our own attitude, the attitude of others changes too. Stick at it and you will see that it works, I promise!

And what a wonderful lesson to teach your kids!

So it goes like this: If you want to attract someone into your life then be the kind of person you want to attract. If you want more respect, then act as if you are worthy of respect by respecting yourself and others. If you want other people to love you, then you need to begin not only by loving others, but by loving yourself first, and *that's* what the next section is all about.

---

[4]Borg, John. "Body Language: 7 Easy Lessons to Master the Silent Language". Albert Mehrabian http://en.wikipedia.org/wiki/Albert_Mehrabian

PART 4

The Third Pillar of

Life-Confidence:

elf-Love

*"You yourself, as much as anybody in the entire universe,
deserve your love & affection"*
Buddha

Chapter 13

What is Self-Love?

"Learning to love yourself is the greatest love of all"

Michael Masser and Linda Creed

Self-Worth
Self-Esteem
Self-Image
Unconditional Love

Are you worth loving? Are you truly worth loving?

Of course you are!

But do *you* love you?

True life-confidence – the kind of life-confidence which separates those who are great achievers from those who merely dream – has one important quality. In the words of Wayne Dyer, it's this: *"A strong, self-image immunity to the fear of criticism and making mistakes"*.

The number one reason for not doing something we would love to do is the fear of failure, and fear of failure is tied up with the need for the good opinion of other people.

To build the necessary confidence – that 'have a go' attitude – where we are not afraid of what people might think if we make a mistake, we need to do one crucial thing before all others. That one thing, quite simply, is this: WE NEED TO LOVE OURSELVES.

In other words – we need to be our own best friend.

When we have sufficient self-love we are then fully equipped to deal with all the challenges life throws at us and what's more, we will attract into our lives the people who we need to help us on our journey.

So let me explain what I mean by self-love. Some of you may feel uncomfortable with the concept of loving yourself, equating it to being conceited and egotistical. This is most definitely not what I mean.

Loving yourself is all about feeling a worthy member of society, a fully functioning human being worthy of respect. Without this self-love you can't possibly hope to be self-confident because you will sub-consciously believe yourself unworthy of other people's love.

- When you love yourself you will feel worthy

- When you love yourself you will feel capable

- When you love yourself you will be authentic

- When you love yourself you will be true to yourself

- When you love yourself you will love other people

- When you love yourself other people will love you

So – to love yourself and to receive love from others you need to make yourself into somebody worth loving. Being respectful of the feelings of others and doing a good turn whenever you can is a good start. Things like keeping your word; not gossiping; being non-judgemental; acknowledging the kindness of others; being on time – all help to make you feel good about yourself.

On the subject of being on time: I have a horse, and every month or so she has to be shod. Farriers seem to have a reputation for never being on time, so I have a special appreciation for my own farrier Steve who is never ever late. *"I don't do late!"* he always says, and if he has to wait longer than ten minutes for someone he goes home!

I was talking to him about this the other day and telling him how much I appreciated his punctuality and he gave me an interesting take on tardiness. He said that when you are late for an appointment with someone, you are actually implying that your time is more important than theirs.

I thought about this for a while and actually it's perfectly true – you are totally disrespecting them. Since this realisation my own punctuality has greatly improved and I undoubtedly feel a more worthy person for it.

It's the many little improvements like this which combine to make you into a better person. A person worthy of love.

For children it's things like sharing, saying thank you, being helpful, comforting another child when they are sad, allowing others to have their turn, learning to be a good loser in games. All these things will help to make them feel worth loving – increasing their self-belief and building their self-esteem, self-image and self-worth. In other words building their life-confidence!

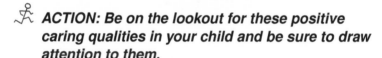 **ACTION: Be on the lookout for these positive caring qualities in your child and be sure to draw attention to them.**

Self-love then is a combination of a strong sense of self-worth and self-esteem and a positive self-image all rolled into one.

Let's just look at these qualities more closely for a moment:

Self-Worth

Self-worth embodies a feeling of being worthy of all the good that comes your way in life. This feeling of worthiness stems from nurturing those good qualities and values within yourself as mentioned above: respect for others, integrity, compassion, consideration, love etc. This makes you more 'lovable' to yourself and in turn raises your sense of self-worth.

People who have a high sense of self-worth accept compliments gracefully. They receive gifts with a sense of worthiness rather than a sense of guilt, and they have the same attitude towards money.

They acknowledge that they are equal to all other human beings, that their feelings are deserving of respect and that they deserve their place on this planet. They are their own best friend.

A good test of the level of your self-worth is to ask yourself, *"Am I my true self in anybody's company?"*

One of my favourite affirmations is, *"If I want to be free, I've got to be me"*

To some degree we all adjust our persona according to who we are with – it's all part of this ingrained human need for the approval of others. However, to repeat the paradox mentioned earlier in the section About This Book – the irony is that the more relaxed we can be and the more we allow our true self to come through, the more powerful we become and the more we command the respect of others!

Self-Esteem

Self-Esteem is vital to life-confidence. Self-esteem is feeling good about yourself and your accomplishments. Each time you achieve a goal through your own efforts your self-esteem is strengthened and you are then likely to go on to build success upon success. People with high self-esteem and self-worth are true to themselves. They are not easily knocked down by negative criticism.

Self-Image

Your self-image is your interpretation of the image you are presenting to the rest of the world – the way you see yourself. It is the perception you have of your appearance, your abilities and your personal qualities, so a strong self-image is a big boost to life-confidence.

To expand on these qualities further we can say that people with poor life-confidence will feel inferior, and be sensitive to criticism (low self-worth). They will feel weak and ineffectual (weak self-esteem). They will put themselves down and find fault with everything about themselves (poor self-image) and they will be afraid to try new things for fear of failure (low self-belief).

Confident people on the other hand will feel equal to anyone and have a strong immunity to criticism (high self-worth). They will hold themselves in high regard (strong self-esteem). They will see themselves as worthy of attention (good self-image) and they will be decisive and unafraid of 'having a go' (high self-belief).

Unconditional Love

An important parenting quality which will provide the foundation for all the above qualities in your child is unconditional love. Every time you demonstrate unconditional love for your child you give them an anchor, a root system from which to grow their confidence.

 ACTION: To ensure your children have the necessary self-love to build their confidence it is crucial that you constantly nurture in them the qualities mentioned above. This means providing them with a positive, supportive environment full of praise and encouragement, which I talk about in the section on Belief. Suffice to say, look upon this as the ongoing, never ending role of a parent or carer.

As with all the strategies in this book, this is not just a tool to use when necessary, but rather a habit, a way of being designed to 'rub off' on them, rather than to teach them.

Life-confidence then, comes from making yourself into someone worth loving, which means being in control of the kind of person you are and taking responsibility for your actions. Managing your feelings and the feelings of others plays a big part in this, and that's what I'm going to talk about next.

Chapter 14

EQ vs IQ

What is EQ? and Why is it More Important Than IQ?
Managing Your Feelings – Developing Self Awareness
The Universal Law of Polarity
Making Friends With Your Fears
The S Factor
Relaxation
More About Visualisation
Meditation
Managing Guilt
The Green Monster
Controlling Anger
Reacting versus Responding

What is EQ and Why is it More Important Than IQ?

The term Emotional Intelligence is something I predict you will be hearing a lot more about in the future. Although still new to many people, Emotional Intelligence for children has actually been around for a while but, as with many new concepts, it necessitates a change in thinking – letting go of old conditioning around how we approach education – and human nature being as it is, that doesn't happen overnight.

With a concept as powerful as this however, there is only so long it can be ignored and I'm pleased to say that, slowly but surely, Emotional Intelligence is beginning to filter its way into schools.

Our Intelligence Quotient (IQ) is a measurement of our intelligence which takes place in the thinking part of the mind i.e. the conscious mind. Our Emotional Quotient (EQ), on the other hand, is to do with our feelings and emotions i.e. the sub-conscious mind.

EQ embraces a whole range of social and emotional competencies. When a child is emotionally competent they are able to manage stress, take responsibility, empathise, manage their feelings, respond to and enhance the feelings of others, make decisions, listen and resolve conflicts.

They will also have a firmly established self-awareness and a strong self-image. EQ levels affect the way children behave, their desire to learn and achieve, their ability to form good relationships, and ultimately their health. Children who have a high EQ will be highly developed in all these areas and this will, in turn, have a direct influence on their level of confidence.

A pioneer of Emotional Intelligence is behavioural scientist Daniel Goleman. Goleman and other proponents of Emotional Intelligence believe that EQ is in fact more important than IQ in ensuring that our children go on to live happy and successful lives.

There is no doubt in my own mind that this is the most important aspect of education your children can ever have, simply because it has such a direct influence upon every other area of life.

Setting and achieving powerful goals in life requires passion, desire, motivation and inspiration, all of which stem from highly developed Emotional Intelligence.

School SATs results are not a reliable gauge of future success. Goleman states that in fact IQ contributes around a mere 20% towards determining a person's success in life[5]. EQ, on the other hand, by its very nature, is all about nurturing self-confidence and motivation which will have a far greater impact on the pursuit of happiness and success.

In addition, the knock-on effect of a high EQ in children, is a greater desire and ability to focus on learning!

---

[5]"Emotional Intelligence: Why it Can Matter More Than IQ", Daniel Goleman

Emotional Intelligence is, without doubt, the most crucial area of development needed to build life-confidence and achieve life-success yet, paradoxically, it is the least taught!!

This is where you come in! I shall now cover the social and emotional competencies you can teach your children.

Managing Your Feelings – Developing Self Awareness

The skill of co-operating and getting along with others involves being able to empathise with their feelings and to do this we first need to be able to recognise, acknowledge and manage our own feelings.

The child who is self-aware and has an understanding of his own feelings, will be far more considerate of the feelings of others and will therefore stand a much better chance of building successful relationships.

Children who have confidence and good self-esteem are more able to deal with their feelings effectively. Nevertheless feelings of anger, jealousy, worry, stress, fear, frustration can all seem overwhelming to a child and teaching them ways to manage these feelings helps them to stay in control.

They need to know that, whilst it's desirable to be able to express our emotions, to live in a civilised society we need to manage them – and feeling-management is a skill which can be learnt.

Children should also be made aware that we all experience negative emotions at times – they are a necessary part of life – and it's important for them to know that this is normal and that feelings don't stay the same for long.

Feelings need to be talked about, not bottled up. Some children may be in denial and try to cover up their feelings whilst others may need help with verbalising how they feel. Younger children particularly will not know how to put their feelings into words.

Talking about how we feel when we are stressed, worried, upset, jealous, afraid or frustrated helps to bring those feelings to the surface. This brings relief and develops our self-awareness, enabling us to manage and control our emotions, keeping them at a level where they do not cause harm.

Children also need to feel understood and empathising with their feelings goes a long way towards helping to dissipate them.

Self-aware children take ownership of their feelings. They are more able to cope because they have learnt to recognise the signs at the onset of an emotion and so channel it in an appropriate way without becoming overwhelmed by it.

On the other hand, children who are never encouraged to acknowledge their feelings will always have a lack of self-awareness. They will be easily overwhelmed by their emotions and unable to manage them. This has a serious effect on their ability to manage their lives, allowing others to control them. Also if they are unable to understand their own feelings, they will fail to understand the feelings of others and this lack of empathy paves the way for a lifetime of dysfunctional relationships.

Suffice to say then, feeling-management is crucial. It is known as Emotional Competence and is at the core of Emotional Intelligence forming the foundation upon which all other EQ aspects are built.

The Universal Law of Polarity

Before I go on to talk about ways to help your children to manage their feelings I want to introduce you to something which, when I first realised how it could benefit my life, blew me away! It would be remiss of me to talk about managing feelings without sharing this crucial life-tool with you.

There is a Universal Law of Polarity, or Law of Opposites which means that everything has an opposite, and the extent to which you utilise this law and integrate it into your everyday life will determine how fulfilled and balanced a life you will lead.

The Law of Polarity states that every positive energy has an equal and opposite negative energy, and every negative energy has an equal and opposite positive energy.

I first learnt the impact of applying this law to everyday life when attending a workshop run by Dr John Demartini called *'The Break-through Experience'.* Dr Demartini writes at length about how you can apply the Law of Polarity to obtain inner peace and calm in your life. In my opinion he is one of the world's greatest speakers on personal growth, and if you ever get a chance to hear him speak I highly recommend you do.

The essence of his message is this: Every circumstance you come across in life will have both benefits and drawbacks in equal pro-portions. To maintain equilibrium in any situation you need to be consciously aware of both the positive and the negative side.

Now, when you're in the midst of a particularly challenging situation it's not always easy to think of how that situation is benefiting you, but if you think hard enough I promise you that, however big the challenge, you will always find benefits!

And conversely, good experiences will always have their drawbacks! Like the north and south poles of a magnet, it's impossible to have one without the other.

The problem is this: Most of us allow ourselves to be carried along by our emotions and consequently we can be on a 'high' one minute and on a 'low' the next – up and down like a yo-yo.

The trick is this: When you're experiencing something negative in your life get into the habit of asking yourself, "What are the benefits of this?" and keep asking that question until you find at least ten benefits or until your emotions begin to feel on more of an even keel and more centred.

Conversely, when you are in a good situation and are on a high, ask the question "What are the drawbacks to this?" and there will be many!

The point is that whenever we are on a high, as sure as the tide changes, it will be followed by a low – and vice versa! However, when we neutralise our emotions by directing our attention to the corresponding benefits or drawbacks, we become grounded and in control and (back to that bicycle metaphor) we become balanced.

   ACTION: I invite you to embrace the Law of Polarity in your everyday life. Begin to live it. Introduce it to your children. Get them to think of the benefits of any negative situation – then watch for the magic to happen!

So now let's take a look at the main negative emotions which we all have to deal with and the many ways in which you can help both yourself and your children to deal with them.

Making Friends With Your Fears

Fear can be caused by a myriad of situations and feelings and there are an equal number of ways of dealing with it.

When we feel fearful our bodies release adrenaline and hormones, these make the heart beat faster, the brain becomes more alert and our muscles tense up. All these physical reactions are nature's way of getting us ready to act.

When faced with danger, an animal has what we know as the 'fight or flight' response. They either stand their ground and fight or else they leg it! Either way they get into definite action.

Of course these are life or death situations and thankfully we humans don't come across many of them, but the same principle applies when dealing with fear in our everyday lives.

That principle is: Fear is dissipated by action. Doing nothing only makes the fear build up. That knot in your stomach pulls tighter and tension permeates into every cell in your body.

When most people think of the word fear they think of being petrified. Fear has many shades of grey however and in fact whenever we are worrying about something, however small, we are actually in a state of fearfulness.

In her excellent book *"Feel the Fear and Do It Anyway"* Susan Jeffers points out that fear is a part of life and that when we face up to a particular fear or worry and act on it, we eventually lose our fear and the task in hand becomes second nature to us.

There will always be another fear just around the corner however, and that next fear will stretch us just that little bit more, and that's how we grow (more about your stretch zone in Chapter 17).

Conquering fear is a bit like a child learning to walk. To begin with they are shaky, but with each step they feel a little surer until eventually it becomes natural and familiar. It's the same with fear. Children should be helped to dissipate their fears through action.

All childhood fears, however trivial they may seem to you, should be taken seriously. They are very real to the child and when fears are dismissed as silly or unimportant children can become very insecure.

 ACTION: Allow time to listen to what your child has to say. Help them to verbalise their feelings and make them feel understood. Talk through a challenge together and come up with a plan of action. Take their concerns seriously, however trivial they may seem.

Children need to learn that we all have fears, even grown ups, and the only way to deal with them is to confront whatever is making us feel afraid – without delay.

There are valuable lessons to be learnt from facing up to our fears, namely:

- Things are rarely as bad as we imagine they are going to be.
- It feels good when we have faced our fears, and...
- Next time we are in a similar situation we will be less fearful.

The S Factor

S is for Stress. Stress is a part of life, and a certain amount of stress is unavoidable. However we need to learn how to manage our stress level to avoid it affecting our health. (You can read more about managing stress in my eBook – *"The Stress Busters"*)

The kind of stress that is undesirable is 'stress build-up'. In other words, it's stress which is allowed to fester and is not dissipated through action. When we allow stress to build up we set ourselves up for problems.

Worry around some unfinished business or necessary action, which is not acted upon, causes this build up of stress. Whilst a certain level of stress is good for keeping us 'on the ball' and performing at our best, too much stress is bad for us.

Some people deal with the issue of stress by trying to avoid it altogether (flight response). Avoiding certain stressful situations before they happen can be a good route to take. But, as with fear, if we are going to grow we can't avoid stress altogether. That leaves us with facing our stress (fight response).

The good news is – the amount of stress we suffer is entirely within our control.

Like all feelings, stress is intrinsically influenced by our thoughts. So first and foremost, we need to recognise that stress is caused by the way we interpret situations in our lives, not by the situations themselves.

Stress is a reaction to a situation and a feeling of not being in control of our lives, and both these factors can be controlled by changing the way we think and the way we act.

Sometimes stress is directly linked to another person, in which case we may need to take steps to involve them in the solution. Respecting our own feelings and being honest with the person involved is a good start. Explaining how we feel and asking for their co-operation is also a step in the right direction (feel the fear). If this isn't appropriate, we should talk to someone else about it to help us clarify what needs to be done.

Very often stress is self-inflicted. By that I mean it is brought about by taking on too many things at once and ending up with 'too many balls in the air', thus having to cope with stress from multiple sources – we've all been there at some time. When you find yourself in this situation you need to recognise, very early on, that something's got to go.

To deal with this you need to prioritise actions and focus on one thing at a time. Writing down a plan of action, a priority list or a timetable will often help you to regain the feeling of being in control.

Break down a busy schedule into daily tasks and take one day at a time. Tackle each task single-mindedly and make sure you see it through to completion before going on to the next.

Cancelling the least important engagements to free up time for top priority ones can bring immediate relief and will restore your control over the situation. Contrary to what I said about the word 'No' earlier, this a time when it's a useful word to have in your vocabulary! Learn to be assertive. Say 'No' to taking on too many commitments.

At other times, stress overload is caused by having to cope with a number of unavoidable circumstances imposed upon us from outside. Again we have to remind ourselves that we can only focus on one thing at time.

Meditation, Visualisation and Relaxation time (however short) will also help to calm and focus the mind (see later in this Chapter). Whether you choose to act on changing the way you look at a situation or whether you choose to act on addressing the people/person involved or whether you do both, there is one indisputable fact:

You must act. And you must act sooner rather than later.

As with fear, the longer you put off dealing with your stress level, the more it builds up, and the more immobilised you become. The more immobilised you become the more difficult it is to act and the more detrimental it is to your health and wellbeing.

The same thing applies to our children. They need to learn that the way to deal with any stressful situation is to go to work on dissipating the stress as soon as possible – and if they leave it too long it will almost certainly get worse.

ACTION: Look out for signs of stress with your children. It may be blatantly obvious such as tearfulness or moodiness, but other signs may not be so easy to spot as they could be wrongly misinterpreted. Take time to do things together. This will open up opportunities to get the communication flowing.

Signs such as refusing to talk; becoming introverted; complaining of feeling unwell; not wanting to go to school, all need to be investigated, and it is important to encourage your child to talk about their feelings and to open up. This should be done tactfully, as a barrage of questions may make them clam up even more.

As mentioned earlier, children may need help with verbalising their problem. Putting your feelings into words is a learned skill and you may have to help them to give their feelings a name. This can often be the trigger to get them to talk more about it.

Take the following example:

Parent: *"I notice you haven't asked if Robyn can come round this week"*

Child: *"I'm not friends with her any more"*

Parent: *"Oh dear, what happened?"*

Child: *"She keeps borrowing my pens without asking and she lost one of them."*

Parent: *"Oh no! That must be annoying. I bet you feel really frustrated too when you need a pen and it's not there"*

Child: *"I do"*

They can then talk through how to deal with it.

However, when you discuss the solution avoid the trap of being too directive. Firstly, children are very inventive and often come up with ideas that you may not have thought of. Secondly, if you encourage them to come up with their own solution they will feel more comfortable with it. Thirdly, you will be encouraging them to take responsibility for their life (see Chapter 14 on Responsibility).

Here are two versions of how the above conversation could continue. The first is directive and leaves no room for input from the child. The second is collaborative and helps the child to have ownership of the solution:

Version 1 The Directive Approach

Parent: *"I think I'll have a word with Mrs Dyer about that"*

Child: *"No I don't want you to"*

Parent: *"Well I shall certainly talk to Robyn's mum at the end of the day, those pens cost a lot of money"*

Version 2 The Collaborative Approach

Parent: *"What have you done about it?"*

Child: *"I asked Robyn to stop taking them but she didn't listen"*

Parent: *"What else do you think you could do?"*

Child: *"Well I could make sure I put my pens away in my bag when I'm not using them"*

Parent: *"Good idea. What else could you do?"*

Child: *"I could leave some pens at home and just take in the ones I use"*

Parent: *"Mmmmm. What else?"*

Child: *"I could tell Mrs Dyer"*

Parent: *"Which one of those things are you going to do?"*

Child: *"I think I'll just take two pens and make sure I put them away"*

(Pause to give child thinking time)

Child: *"And if that doesn't work I'll tell Mrs Dyer"*

Here are a couple more scenarios and stress avoidance solutions:

Example 1

Your child is worried that he may not being able to do a certain sum in maths.

Stress avoidance: Child asks the teacher for help.

Parent helps child to practise sums.

Parent sees teacher.

Example 2

Your child has broken her friend's ruler and she is afraid she won't be friends any more.

Stress avoidance: Child tells her friend about it and says sorry.

Child buys her friend a new ruler.

Child rings her friend up to apologise.

Parent rings friend's mother to apologise.

Although stress shouldn't be allowed to build up, if the stress is brought about by a conflict with another person, just as with anger it is better to allow some time for emotions to settle, and only talk to the people concerned when you are in a calm rational state.

> *ROLE MODEL: Whenever the opportunity arises you can demonstrate the importance of talking about feelings by talking about your own feelings. Keep the conversation light however. The purpose here is to role model the necessity of acknowledging our feelings, not to unburden our feelings onto our children.*

Familiarising yourself with the strategies throughout this book, to help your children build their confidence and self-image, will be a good buffer when they find themselves under stress.

Relaxation

You won't need me to tell you that children are 'on the go' from morning till dusk – and then some. Taking time together to be calm and to practise relaxing can be very beneficial in reducing stress, and helping to focus and concentrate.

There are a variety of things you can say to get children into a relaxed state whilst at the same time relaxing yourself.

Examples:

Sit comfortably and close your eyes. Imagine a warm sunbeam of light shining down on you and making your body feel lovely and warm. And as the sunbeam flows through your body you feel it taking all your worries away and you begin to relax. The sunbeam flows through your arms, and they begin to feel heavy. Just let them go. It goes down through your hands and your fingers feel warm and relaxed. You can feel the warm sun, going through your body down through your legs right through to your toes. Now you feel warm all over, warm, heavy and relaxed.

Another way to get children to relax is to tell them to talk to their bodies. They sit quietly with their eyes closed and think 'Toes go to sleep' and feel all the tension draining away from their toes. Moving up the body they do the same with the legs, fingers, hands, arms, shoulders, eyes, jaw until they are completely relaxed.

Children find it difficult to completely relax at first because they cannot recognise tension in their bodies. To help them you can ask them to first scrunch up their toes, for example, and then let them relax. This will help them to notice the difference.

As with anything else, practice makes perfect. You can help them by making this a sort of game. Get them to lie down and when you have talked them through relaxing each part of the body test them by lifting their leg or arm a little way off the floor and then letting it go. It should flop to the ground. Then let them test you!

More About Visualisation

Earlier I talked about the power of visualisation (see Chapter 12). Guided Visualisation can help children to cope with a variety of situations such as stress, anxiety, bereavement, exam nerves, and hyperactivity and it can also be used to great effect to improve academic performance.

One particular visualisation I have found to be very effective with children and adults alike is one I call 'The Secret Place'.

I first put on some relaxing music and I ask the children to sit comfortably, usually in a chair, and to rest their arms on their legs, palms up.

I then ask them to close their eyes and talk them through the process of becoming completely relaxed (see above). I then explain that I am going to show them a way of getting rid of all their worries.

I tell them that, in their mind, I want them to go to a special, secret place where they will feel safe and happy. This special place can be somewhere they have been before like a garden or somewhere they visited on holiday, or it can be a place they make up.

I then ask them to imagine what this place is like using all their senses:

What can they see? Bright coloured flowers? Trees to climb? Boats on the sea? Swings and slides? etc.

What can they hear? The sound of the sea? Birds singing? Laughter? Fairground music? etc.

What can they feel? The wind on their cheeks? The warm sand between their toes? The sun? The cool sea? A duvet wrapped around them? etc.

What can they smell or taste? Ice cream? Perfumed flowers? Hot dogs cooking? A bonfire? The smell of the sea? The salty taste?

When working with individual children you can find out from them first where they'd like to be and then make your visualisation more specific and personalised.

Explain that this is a place where they are really safe and when they go there all their worries disappear. They are in charge of who they allow into their secret place. They may be alone or they may want their mum or dad, best friend, pet or favourite toy with them.

They then sit quietly for a while thinking of their special place and building up a picture in their mind.

It's important not to rush this bit. When the brain is in a relaxed, alpha brain-wave state, as in light meditation, 5 minutes can seem like just a few seconds.

I then tell them that, when they are ready, they can leave their secret place and come back into the room. At this point I find children are very reluctant to open their eyes because they are having such a great time!

When they are all 'back' I explain that they can go to their secret place anytime they wish. They can go there to help them get to sleep at night and, whenever they are feeling sad or worried, the magic of the secret place will help them to cope with their feelings.

Once in their secret place they can use their imagination to visualise themselves coping and succeeding with any problem they may have.

The above is a lovely exercise which I have done often and when children are familiar with this visualisation they can change from an active lively state into a relaxed one very quickly, empowering them to take control of their own feelings.

Meditation

Certain kinds of stress like the death of a pet or family member cannot be avoided. However, children should be made aware that whilst some situations are out of our control there are ways of helping us cope with them.

More and more people are turning to meditation in these stressful times. Those who practise Yoga for example will know how helpful meditation can be. Children are particularly receptive to this form of stress-relief. Meditation is a recharging of your batteries. It's nothing more than giving yourself space to quietly clear the mind of that voice in your head which never stops talking – usually feeding you negative, limiting beliefs.

To help yourself do this you first need to get into a relaxed state and then focus your attention on a single object or sound. Focussing on your breathing is one way of doing this.

There are many different ways of meditating. Many people meditate whilst listening to music, some like sitting in the garden and listening to the birds; going for a walk or a run; becoming absorbed in some sort of craft; singing; playing an instrument, it's very individual. There are many things which can be used as a focus to rid ourselves temporarily of that incessant voice in our heads.

Again, meditation becomes easier the more we practise it and it can be extremely energising and rejuvenating.

Managing Guilt

Being so eager to please and fit in, kids often have feelings of guilt. As well as helping them to talk about it, they need plenty of unconditional love and reassurance to help them deal with these feelings.

Children can also feel guilty about other people's problems, especially close family. For this reason, whilst it is desirable and indeed necessary for children to realise that everyone experiences the same emotions as them, parents need to be mindful of expressing their emotions too dramatically in front of their children.

Children often feel responsible for the way their parents are feeling. Arguments; separation; divorce; illness – these are all examples of situations when children can feel they are to blame, and they will need reassurance that it's not their fault. Always be aware of this and take care not to expose them to aggressive arguments.

The Green Monster

Jealousy is another destructive emotion and needs to be dealt with as soon as it raises its ugly head. The seed of jealousy is insecurity and lack of self-worth. Jealousy can take on all sorts of forms, from moodiness to aggression, and foster various kinds of behaviour, from refusing to leave your side to downright destructiveness.

Whether it's being jealous of a new partner or a sibling or new baby, your child needs to be helped to cope with this green-eyed monster.

Although a certain amount of jealousy is inevitable at times, there is a lot which can be done to avoid jealous feelings arising, and your children will be better equipped to deal with this emotion if you have helped them to build self-confidence and a strong sense of self-worth from an early age.

Here are some basic ground rules for staving off jealousy:

Be Fair

With sibling rivalry it's important to be able to empathise with the feelings of both children. Avoid always blaming the older child just because the younger one is too young to know any different. When the youngest child does something unkind make sure you say so.

Make Time

Taking time to spend with your children individually is so important and making that time, in spite of a busy workload, will pay dividends.

Young babies, disabled or sick children can demand a lot of attention, but making time for other siblings is absolutely necessary if you want to avoid problems with jealousy. Enlisting the help of a partner, family member or friend may be what is needed here.

Put Feelings Into Words

Strong negative feelings can be overwhelming for a small child and, as I mentioned earlier, they are often unable to verbalise how they feel. You can stave off feelings of jealousy by verbalising their feelings for them.

For example:

"You must be feeling fed up waiting for mummy to finish feeding your brother"

or *"You must have felt angry when your sister took your pens"*.

Putting feelings into words helps in many ways: it relieves the frustration and confusion caused by not understanding what's happening; it helps children to feel accepted; it reassures them; above all it helps them to feel understood.

Acknowledge Kindnesses

Noticing when your child behaves kindly towards the object of their jealousy, and at the same time, actually telling them you have noticed and praising them, is a positive reinforcement of their behaviour.

Controlling Anger – Responding versus Reacting

Anger causes stress and when we are angry we want to employ the fight response.

When our emotions are running high we instinctively react to a situation and are therefore not in control of what we say. When we are calm and in control of our emotions, instead of reacting we *respond* to it. Children need to realise that reacting, i.e. expressing your anger to someone in an uncontrolled way, will only make the problem worse.

It's never a good idea to deal with a situation when we are angry. In this reactive state we will either say things we don't mean or else we will express what we mean in an unconstructive way, either way we usually make the situation worse and then regret it later.

We can experience a variety of stressful emotions when we are in conflict with someone or feel we have been unfairly treated: Humiliation; shock; embarrassment; frustration; fear; regret – all these emotions can be very strong. In a conflict situation, what then often happens is those initial feelings then turn to feelings of anger, indignation and resentment.

There will always be times when anger raises its ugly head. Children's emotions can flare up at the flick of a switch and they then become 'stuck in the moment' and blocked from moving forward.

To avoid losing control children need to practise recognising the feelings which precede anger. They then need to practise expressing those primary feelings by verbalising them in a more controlled way instead of becoming angry. They will then come to realise that this is by far the most effective way to deal with conflict.

 Unlike other emotions, when encouraging children to talk about their anger we must be careful not to 'fan the flames' and make them worse. Tread gingerly and wait for the right moment. An angry child may need a cooling down period before they can talk about the way they feel.

Once anger has set in, two things need to happen initially before you can begin to unravel arguments.

- First the child needs to deal with their anger.
- Second they need to break away from the 'blame mindset'

First let's look at how to deal with the anger:

Choose a time to talk about anger management when your child is calm and receptive, perhaps when you are doing something together. Make it clear to your child that it's OK to get angry feelings – that's normal – but it's how we deal with those feelings that counts.

Explain to him that when you want to solve a problem that has made you angry you will get much better results when you get your anger out of the way first. If you try and solve things when you're angry it's your anger that's solving it, not you, and 'Anger' is useless at solving problems, it's only good at making things worse!

When dealing with a recent incident, get them to think of how they were feeling when they began to get angry. What was their body feeling like? Was their heart beating faster? What were they thinking? What were they doing at the time? Were they feeling tense? Breathing faster? What was the other person doing? Developing this awareness is the first step towards recognising the warning signs – the signals that say it's time to walk away and buy some time to calm down.

 Children's emotions can flare up at the flick of a switch and it can be helpful for them to have a 'secret signal' at the ready to help them recognise those feelings that precede an angry outburst.

This signal may be a trigger word or phrase they say in their head such as 'Out' 'Stop' 'Switch' 'Chill' 'Time out', or it could be something they visualise, like a red light that goes on in their head, or a pause button they press on the back of their hand.

Ask them for suggestions for their secret signal. Children will come up with great ideas once they know what's needed and when they work out their own strategy it has a greater chance of working because it's personal to them.

When they next feel themselves getting angry they can then take themselves away from the situation long enough to calm down. Time out for a minimum of twenty minutes to half an hour is needed to cool down, and longer according to the strength of the emotion.

Once they have walked away from a conflict, children, just like adults, benefit from thinking about a specific cooling down strategy to use to deal with their anger. Some sort of physical activity such as going for a run; punching a pillow etc. is a great antidote to anger, as is humour such as reading a comic or watching a humorous cartoon.

Having calmed down they are then in a responsive frame of mind rather than a reactive one and are more able to go about finding a solution in a constructive way rather than a destructive one.

Life is all about relationships. Being in harmony with other people is instrumental in achieving success of any kind. The ability to avoid conflicts and to be able to resolve them in a positive way when they do arise, is an indispensible life-skill for children to learn. For this reason I have devoted the whole of the next chapter to this subject.

Chapter 15

How To Make Yourself Worth Loving

Building Good Relationships – People Who Need People
Honouring the Values of Others
Solve the Problem – Resolve the Conflict
An Opportunity to Grow
Breaking Away From Blame
The Magic of the Talking Stick
Dean's Story

Building Good Relationships – "People Who Need People"

People need people. How happy and successful we are has a direct correlation with how well we interact with others. Whatever we choose to do in life will in some way involve relationships, so it stands to reason that the person who is able to empathise with, understand, interpret and respond positively to the feelings of others, has a head start on the road to success.

Whilst children need to learn positive ways of dealing with disputes and resolving conflicts, which I shall deal with later, the ultimate aim as they get older is for them to acquire the skill of avoiding conflict altogether.

In his book *"The 7 Habits of Highly Effective People"*, Stephen Covey uses a wonderful metaphor. He talks about building good relationships by building up an 'Emotional Bank Account'. By this he means keeping commitments, doing kindnesses, being understanding, showing integrity and being honest.

Each time you demonstrate one of these qualities, Covey equates it to making a deposit into the person's Emotional Bank Account. He says we need to build up this 'account' to the point where it will withstand the odd 'withdrawal' e.g. showing impatience; being late for an appointment etc. However, if your 'withdrawals' outnumber your 'deposits' then the friendship won't last.

We can apply this concept to your relationship with yourself:

I believe that loving yourself is all about building up your own 'Emotional Bank Account' . When you work on having high integrity, being caring, giving of yourself, being true to your word, keeping commitments and nurturing all the qualities which you personally value highly, you will find yourself very easy to love!

You can help your child to build her own 'Emotional Bank Account' with herself by drawing attention to her qualities and considerate actions.

 ACTION: *See how many times over the next week you can 'catch your child being good' or doing something helpful or positive. When you do, make sure you point it out to her and praise her for it. Now extend that week to 30 days. By then you will have established a firm habit of looking out for the positive behaviour. Play the Emotional Bank Account game with your child and watch her sense of self-worth and self-love soar.*

Honouring the Values and Opinions of Others

In Chapter 12 I talked about values in the context of helping children to achieve their goals. Taking this a stage further, in the context of relationships children need to be helped to recognise and acknowledge the values of others. Whilst you can't impose your own values onto someone else, you can develop the skill of building rapport with others by linking their values with your own.

Here's an example:

If buying a new car was high on your list of values and controlling finances and saving money was a high value for your partner, you can see how there could be potential conflict.

If however you researched the savings you would make on fuel economy, cheaper insurance, repair bills etc compared to your old car, and presented a summary of this to your partner, you would now be much more in harmony with his or her values.

We often do this value-negotiating instinctively, but it is at those times when our emotions begin to take over, that we need to make a conscious effort to remember to acknowledge the other person's values.

Learning to recognise the values of others and honouring those values is a powerful tool in the building of harmonious relationships and avoiding conflicts. For children of course this is an advanced skill to learn, but as they get older you can introduce this concept to them.

Solve the Problem – Resolve the Conflict

SOLUTION FOCUSED

In order to move forward towards the solution to any problem, it is necessary to become solution focused. This may seem obvious but so often we become entrenched in the problem and unable to see the wood for the trees.

Your role as a parent is to help your child to disentangle themselves from the situation and to see themselves as part of the solution instead of part of the problem.

Solving problems is all about considering options. When faced with a problem of any kind the first step is to encourage your children to brainstorm every possible option. This is a skill that must be learnt through practice. Each suggestion should be accepted without judgment, no matter how far-fetched it may sound. It helps at first to write them all down to make it easier to review them.

Once he has a list of options your child can then weigh up the pros and cons and decide which ones he is going to go with; which ones he is going to eliminate; which ones he could come back to if the chosen ones don't work.

From an early age children can be given the opportunity to decide between options – at first between two options, then as they grow older they can cope with a larger number. (See Choices in Chapter 11)

Problem solving needn't always be a long drawn out exercise but it's important to take every opportunity for your child to practise thinking of options and making choices.

An Opportunity to Grow

Although children who have a high EQ will be less likely to become too emotionally involved in arguments, there will inevitably be times when disagreements occur and teaching them how to overcome these will give them an invaluable life-skill.

 When children practise conflict resolution often enough they will automatically begin to avoid conflicts ever arising: Conflict resolution leads to conflict avoidance.

Whilst the aim then is to help children to learn how to avoid getting *into* confrontational situations – first and foremost they need to learn how to get *out* of them.

So what's the best way to deal with arguments?

When your child is in a full blown argument with another child, the easy way out is to say to them, *"If you can't play without quarrelling then keep away from each other".* The easy way out for you that is, because although it may put a temporary halt to the conflict, there's nothing to say it won't recur.

If children come to me ranting, raving and crying about some in-justice each feels the other has done, I welcome it. No I'm not a masochist! I just know that this is a wonderful opportunity for me to help them to grow. So rather than dismissing the situation as a silly squabble, I recognise it for what it is: A chance for them to learn a valuable lesson in developing their communication skills. I welcome this chance with open arms and always give it the time and attention it deserves.

It cannot be overemphasised that time spent on facilitating good communication skills is a worthwhile investment.

 Getting the best out of other people is the greatest skill we can learn. Our success is in direct proportion to how well we interact with others.

Children who learn to consider the feelings of others by respecting their wishes, being true to their word and listening with empathy and understanding, will not only learn the rewards of giving but will also grow to feel they are truly worthy – the foundation for life-confidence.

Breaking Away From Blame

When presented with children in conflict, I first of all talk to each of them separately and listen to each one with understanding.

Even when the arguing has stopped, the angry voice in their head is on full volume and the adrenaline is still rushing through the body and it's then that the 'blame mindset' kicks in.

Once they have had sufficient time out away from each other to calm down, I will get them back together again. I then always begin by saying something like this:

"Right. Now we can't change what's happened. That's gone. The past is past. I'm not interested in you telling me whose fault it was because what happened – happened, and you can't change it. I'm only interested in what happens from now onwards. So what we can do is work out a plan to make sure it never happens again".

In this way I am making them part of the solution not the problem.

Once you have got them to break away from blaming each other, i.e. in responsive mode rather than reactive mode, they are then ready to do 'The Talking Stick' exercise...

The Magic of the Talking Stick

"Never assume that the other person understands you until they feed it back. Never assume that you understand them until you have fed it back"

Brian Tracy

The above quote captures perfectly the essence of the Talking Stick Exercise. It's all about each child empathising with the feelings of the other.

I have used this exercise mainly with Primary School children, but it can be used with all ages with equal effect. It's a combination of conflict resolution skills talked about in the books by Faber and Mazlish and those used by the Native American Indians.

The Native American Indians had a very effective way of resolving conflict situations. They used what is known as a Talking Stick which was a special stick lovingly decorated with feathers, beads, personal mementoes and tokens (and, I suspect maybe the odd skull or two!), bound with leather and greatly revered.

The principle of the Talking Stick exercise is that only the person holding the Talking Stick is allowed to speak.

Children absolutely love the idea of the Talking Stick and when I first introduced it to my class, home-made talking sticks of all shapes, sizes and colours arrived over the next week, without my asking for them!

As they practised using the Talking Stick the children gradually moved from having me as an arbitrator – talking them through the process of the exercise, and refereeing the proceedings – to resolving their conflicts for themselves. We had a special Talking Stick Corner and the whole initiative was a huge success.

I highly recommend you use this exercise. It's a great way to teach children to empathise with the feelings of others and, in turn, when someone else takes the trouble to truly listen to what they themselves have to say, they immediately become calm and their level of self-worth rises..

One thing I would say is this: To be successful you need to follow the rules strictly.

I also suggest you encourage the children to treat the Talking Stick with reverence. Keep it in a special place when not in use and use it strictly for conflict resolution only and not for playing with. In this way it will be respected and you will stand a better chance of success. Reproduced on the next page are the instruction sheets which I use with the children.

Problem Solving Instructions

The Past is the Past

"We cannot put right the past. We can only improve the future"

ALL ARGUING AND BLAMING STOPS HERE!

STAGE 1 Describe How You Feel

PERSON A. . . Hold the Talking Stick and describe what happened and how it made you feel.

PERSON B. . . Hold the Talking Stick and repeat what Person A has said until they feel understood.

PERSON B. . . Hold the Talking Stick and describe what happened and how it made you feel.

PERSON A. . . Hold the Talking Stick and repeat what Person B has said until they feel understood.

STAGE 2 Brainstorm Options

PERSON A and PERSON B think of a long list of what could be done in the future to stop the problem arising again. All options should be written down even if you don't agree with them. **No 'Ifs and Buts'!** Any comment or discussion at this stage is strictly against the rules.

STAGE 3 Decide on Options

PERSON A and PERSON B now discuss the options and decide which ones are agreeable to both parties. Write the agreed options down and keep the list to remind you. **SHAKE HANDS.**

Indian Talking Stick Rules

Solve your problems here

STAGE 1 When describing how you feel:

- Only the one who is holding the talking stick is allowed to speak

- Each person must feel understood before you continue

STAGE 2 When brainstorming options:

- All suggestions must be allowed

- BE CAREFUL! No one is allowed to discuss, argue, criticise or disagree at this stage

STAGE 3 When deciding which options to keep:

- Each option must be agreeable to all concerned

- NEVER come away without an agreement

- If you can't reach an agreement ask an adult for help

The Talking Stick is a great bonding exercise for all the family, and practising the habit of empathising with other people makes for far less stress all round.

One client I was coaching held a family workshop and the entire family sat round the table and each made their own talking stick. They each have a special hook where the Talking Sticks hang in a row and are taken down whenever a conflict needs to be resolved.

Although this exercise was initially instigated for the sake of the children, it ended up being beneficial for the relationship of the parents as well!

Adults can, in fact, benefit greatly from the Talking Stick exercise. My husband and I have settled many a 'stale mate' situation by using this method. We don't actually use a Talking Stick per se. In fact the last time we settled a disagreement we were in Starbucks so we used a spoon instead! (I think we would have turned a few heads if we had passed a feathered stick back and forth over the Cappuccinos!)

To demonstrate the efficacy of the Talking Stick exercise with children let me tell you a true story:

Dean's Story

Dean was a little boy who found it very difficult to concentrate. He was constantly calling out and interrupting lessons and was always in the wrong place at the wrong time! He was a delightful little lad, always very open and honest with a certain naivety about him.

Whenever there was trouble afoot Dean was usually at the scene of the crime! He seemed to gravitate towards it, often becoming unwittingly involved in going to someone's rescue and trying to 'sort things out'.

We had been working with the class Talking Stick for some weeks now, but as far as Dean was concerned the squabbling continued. Whilst the social skills of the rest of the class were coming on in leaps and bounds, not a day went by without Dean being involved in some sort of conflict and, try as I may, I just didn't seem to be able to get through to him.

In truth I was feeling very despondent. We were nearing the end of term and I would be leaving my job in a few days and I was beginning to despair of ever getting through to Dean.

It was my very last day. As I was passing the empty classroom at break time I happened to hear voices. I peeped round the door. There was Dean and another boy. They had come into the classroom to get the Talking Stick!

I couldn't believe my eyes and ears! Dean was sitting opposite the other child in the Talking Stick Corner, Talking Stick in hand, looking very serious. Neither of them noticed me at the door.

Totally focused and intently looking the other boy in the eye, Dean was saying,

"So you felt frustrated, sad and angry when I kicked your ball over the fence. I understand how you feel and I'm very sorry. I won't do it again!"

I don't mind telling you I had a lump in my throat!

That's the power of listening to understand!

Chapter 16

Respect – The Parent/Child Relationship

Quality Time With Your Children

Earlier on I said it was not necessary to schedule extra activity time into your day. Well, I lied! Actually I'm only joking! Although what I'm going to talk about now requires you to do a bit of juggling of activities and perhaps forfeiting something of lesser priority, it is certainly possible to do, and the rewards will be well worth it.

What I'm going to ask you to do is this. . .

Spend some quality time with your children – one to one.

I appreciate the fact that parents are busy people and are constantly multi-tasking, and your first thought may well be, *"I just can't afford to spend the time"* My reply to you would be: *"You can't afford not to!"*

Seriously, you really can't afford not to for many reasons – some of which I shall talk about next.

Strengthening the Bond

When a new baby comes into the family, both parents and siblings build a bond with that baby which grows stronger over the years. The problem is, at times life becomes hectic. Your children may be asserting their independence, or pushing your patience to see how far they can go; you may have the stress of a job and other things going on in your life and a day never seems to have enough hours. Life is one big juggling act.

Sound familiar? At these times the bond you have built can get obscured temporarily, which is why it's important to spend one to one time to 'touch base' with your children and affirm your love for them.

If you have more than one child you should try to give some one-to-one time to each one, individually, even the odd 10 minutes is better than nothing. You may have to enlist the help of a partner, friend or family member. It's absolutely crucial to build in time to do fun things with them. Things like sharing a bedtime story, going to the park, playing football, baking cakes, going swimming and many more, are all opportunities for quality time.

Why is it so important? Well, apart from the obvious enjoyment for both parent and child, time spent on enjoying things together will pay dividends in many ways. When quality time is neglected and that bond is obscured, it's easy to lose touch with that mutual respect so important in a relationship of any kind.

And when there is a lack of respect and a lack of mutual understanding of feelings, there is a danger of a breakdown of communication. With children, boundaries are then challenged and behaviour starts to deteriorate.

The pre-teenage years offer the very best opportunity for you to strengthen the bond with your children and also to teach them the life skills they need to survive in this world. An added bonus is it builds the foundation for a stronger relationship with your teenager in the future.

Once they are teenagers, young people will turn to their friends for support with some things but they still need to know you are there for them. At this stage it's a good idea to create opportunities for them to voluntarily share their worries or concerns with you rather than bombarding them with questions. Get into the habit of having family meal times all together when possible and also make time to do things together one-to-one. Going for a walk is somehow far more conducive to a good heart to heart chat than sitting in the living room.

Remember not to fire too many questions at them – let them open up naturally. When they do, make sure you are a good listener – they need your understanding and your undivided attention first and foremost. If they want your advice they'll ask for it. In any case it's far more effective to help them come up with solutions to problems themselves (see Chapter 15 for more about problem solving).

Using Leverage

With young children, when inappropriate behaviour arises, if you have put some regular quality time in place, you can use those fun times as leverage by pointing out that the way your child is acting doesn't make you feel inclined to do good things with him.

⚠ *A word of warning here however. Leverage should be used with sensitivity and not as a bribe or a threat. Quality time should be viewed as something you do because you value and enjoy each other's company. If it is used blatantly as a tool for you to manipulate your child's behaviour you will undermine its true purpose which is to demonstrate your unconditional love and respect.*

Leverage needs to be used with the right intent. In other words, it should be used to foster mutual respect for each other and to develop your child's ability to empathise with other people's feelings. The message being that if you give someone your co-operation you are likely to get theirs in return – a valuable life-lesson, which will stand them in good stead in their future relationships.

If you don't take the time do the enjoyable things with them, you will have no leverage.

A word about bribes and threats:

Whilst it's good to reward your children, avoid using a reward as a bribe to get them to do something.

For example:

"If you help with the dishes I'll give you extra pocket money"

Using bribes can foster a "What's in it for me?" mentality. Children should do things for the right reason, i.e. to be considerate of the feelings of others, and if you sometimes feel like an unpaid servant, it's time for a re-think.

It's a good idea to encourage your children to help around the house from an early age. Getting them into the habit of helping with even small jobs, like tidying their room or laying the table, will foster in them a spirit of fairness and being part of the family team. If they are not in the habit of helping it's much more difficult to get their co-operation when they are older.

Some parents feel that when they rush around doing things for their children they are being a good parent and showing their love. On the contrary, by facilitating your children's development of empathy and consideration for your feelings, you will be helping them to grow up to be caring towards others. What greater way could there be to show your love than that? (See more on encouraging Responsibility in Chapter 11).

Threats can be just as damaging as bribes. There may be occasions when it is appropriate to withdraw privileges and children should be made aware that inappropriate behaviour brings consequences, but try to remain calm at all times. Losing your cool and speaking in a threatening tone of voice can come across as bullying and this is a trait which you don't want to be modelling.

The other problem with threats is, like the words 'No' or 'Don't' (see Chapter 9), they can often be used flippantly. Parents who habitually use threats to control behaviour and never follow through with those threats will eventually render them next to useless because they will no longer be taken seriously. I prefer to use the words 'reminders' or 'warnings'. If your child behaves in an unacceptable way calmly tell them why it is unacceptable and what the consequences will be if it happens again and be prepared to follow through with those consequences.

Keeping to your word will very likely mean that the need to enforce sanctions will diminish because children will take you more seriously and will modify their behaviour to avoid being given that ultimatum.

Respect For Your Feelings

I can't over emphasise how important it is for kids to experience how good it feels to enjoy great times with you. The value of those times will have a strong bearing on their attitude towards you during other times of the day or week and the respect they have for you will grow.

The paradox is that when you invest this time, the resulting co-operation you get from your children will mean you can get your daily chores done so much quicker.

When they see how you 'give' to them by making time for doing fun things, they in turn will be more inclined to 'give' to you in the form of appropriate, helpful behaviour and consideration for your feelings. It's teamwork!

As I discussed earlier – considering the feelings of others is an important aspect of Emotional Intelligence. If your children behave inappropriately at times, which we all do, make sure you tell them how it makes you feel. Children respond to being reminded that you are human and that you have emotions too, much more readily than to being shouted at.

I frequently remind my class how they are making me feel. For example, during a class discussion, if they are busy chatting when they are supposed to be listening I might say something like,

"You know – I'm not feeling very happy inside at the moment. (pause) The reason I'm sitting here is to help you and, when you're not bothering to listen or join in, it makes me feel hurt and sad inside. (pause) It makes me feel like not bothering to help you any more"

The positive response is always instantaneous. It beats yelling and raving hands down. Equally, of course, you should look out for opportunities to tell your kids when they have done something to make you feel good:

"You were so thoughtful when you carried that stuff out for me, thank you, you made me feel really happy!"

Respect For Your Child's Feelings

Do you always respect your child's feelings? It's quite likely that you feel you do. Nevertheless, where feelings are concerned, it's a good idea to constantly remind yourself that children are young adults.

Try this for the next week: Make yourself super aware of how you are relating to your child. Are you speaking to them in a respectful manner?

 Throughout each day whenever you interact with your children ask yourself these questions: "Would I speak like this to an adult?" "Would I behave like this towards an adult?"

Of course children differ from adults in that they are dependent on us for guidance and direction but they are no less deserving of our respect and the bonus is they are far more likely to co-operate if we show it.

You would do well to be constantly asking yourself those two important questions. The different perspective it gives you may well surprise you.

Children Should Be Seen *and* Heard!

When I was a child phrases like *"Children should be seen and not heard"*, and *"Children should know their place"* were instilled into me on a regular basis. It meant that when we were in the company of other adults we were not allowed to talk, or even to move, let alone take part in the conversation!

Thank goodness we don't treat our children like this today! Having said that, sometimes you see behaviour which seems to have gone to the opposite extreme.

Children should be taught to be polite and respectful of other people's feelings. Running amok and being generally loud and infringing on the space of others, particularly in public places, does not come under that remit. Call me old fashioned, but when I am sitting in an eating place and children start running around the tables, playing hide and seek behind my chair, and generally invading my space I am not a happy bunny!

As I mentioned earlier, there is a distinction between precocity and confidence:

Precocity means, *"I am the only important person here"*.

Confidence means, *"I am important but I acknowledge that you are too!"*

Whilst I believe that children should be considerate to others, I also believe however that adults should demonstrate consideration to children! My maxim is: 'Children should be seen *and* heard!' In other words, their presence should be acknowledged.

When in the presence of children, I'm sure most adults have been guilty at some time of 'talking above their heads'. By this I mean talking to each other as if the child were invisible and never including them in the conversation.

I include myself here too – it's so easy to do! Just ask yourself here, if another adult were present would you ignore them? If you did of course, it would be considered rude.

Being oblivious to the fact that children are listening and totally excluding them from the conversation, sends out the message loud and clear that their feelings don't matter to you, they are not really important and they are only worth talking to when there are no adults around.

You don't need to be constantly including your child in the conversation, in fact it would be inappropriate if you did. Just include them enough to respect their feelings and acknowledge they are there.

 ROLE MODEL: To ignore your child's presence completely is belittling and can be bad for their self-esteem and, apart from anything else, how on earth can we expect them to be polite if we demonstrate such sheer bad manners ourselves!

Quality Time for You

As well as setting aside time for your children, spending some quality time with yourself is equally important.

Richard Carlson who wrote *'Don't Sweat the Small Stuff'* and *'Creating Miracles Every Day'* among others, tells of how he books what he calls 'White Time' into his weekly schedule, which is time for himself.

If anyone wishes to arrange a meeting at that time, business or otherwise, he says he's sorry but he already has an appointment. In his eyes this is telling the truth because he has an appointment with himself and, barring absolute emergencies, this appointment with himself is never ever broken.

Acknowledging that you deserve some quality time, will strengthen your sense of self-worth and the relaxation will work wonders for your morale. This 'Me Time' is absolutely necessary for you to relax and recharge your batteries. Here again you may have to enlist the help of another adult with this.

 ACTION: Each week, make that appointment with yourself and block it into your diary. It may be walking the dog, window shopping, reading a good book, soaking in a hot bath, booking a massage or just sitting in front of the television with a glass of wine. Whatever it is – BOOK IT and KEEP TO IT!

 ROLE MODEL: When you spend time with yourself your children will see that you believe it is important to value yourself.

Being an Active Listener in a World That Doesn't Listen

I've talked already about making sure you allow silence for your child to say what they need to say (see Collaboration vs Direction in Chapter 11) and I'd like to elaborate more here on the importance of developing the skill of listening.

Taking an active interest in what others have to say is a skill that has to be learnt – because human beings are essentially self-centred and preoccupied with their own thoughts. Everyone's favourite subject is themselves! The ability to control the urge to talk about yourself and listen to the other person instead comes easier to some people than to others, but if you master it, you are well on your way to forming successful relationships.

Here are some interesting findings:

A study of the communication skills of speaking, writing, reading and listening (Wilt 1950) showed the percentage of time each skill is used – figures which, whilst of no real significance on their own, become hugely significant when coupled with a later study (Burley-Allen 1982) which revealed the amount of time the education system actually allocates to teaching each of those skills. This research remains relevant to today's education system and is still cited by many. It reveals that writing is the most taught literacy skill in our schools (students receive 12 years of formal teaching) and yet it is used in everyday life a mere 9% of the time. A great deal of time is also spent on the teaching of reading (6 – 8 years) but this skill is used just 16% of the time. Speaking is given less attention at school than the former two (merely 1 – 2 years) yet is used 30% of the time. However it is the skill of listening that takes the biscuit! Listening is used in everyday life an enormous 45% of the time – yet it is the least taught of all literacy skills (0 – ½ year)!

Is it any wonder then, that most adults and children alike have poor listening skills?

As adults we are not very good at demonstrating good listening skills to our children, mainly because we have never been taught them ourselves.

Being an active listener means not just hearing what a person is saying but actually understanding the meaning of what they say and also sensing what is *not* being said and responding accordingly.

Making eye contact; noticing tone of voice; picking up on body language; empathising; totally absorbing the actual words spoken – these are all skills of active listening.

Listening games and exercises can be very valuable in helping to develop your child's listening skills. They are also a test of communication skills.

Try these:

- One person describes a picture or pattern in detail and the other person draws what they hear. They then match their drawing up with the original.

- One person is blindfolded and the other gives instructions to get them to the other side of a room around a series of obstacles.

- One person has the outline of an island map and the other then reads out details of exactly where to draw various land-marks like rivers, swamps, trees etc.

- Any problem, instruction or riddle can be presented to a child by reading it out to them instead of them reading it themselves.

- Also the value of story telling cannot be over emphasised. Listening to stories on CDs is also a good activity which is under-used in favour of the TV or computer screen. Children who have a lot of visual stimulus can become lazy listeners.

Parents should always be aware of the quality of their own listening. When you listen actively you are giving your child undivided attention and internalising what they are saying. You are demonstrating that you acknowledge that what they have to say is important to them and deserving of your attention. It makes them feel valued and worthy and is an important ingredient in the life-confidence recipe.

Half-listening, e.g. watching television whilst your child is talking to you; not making eye contact; having your mind preoccupied with something else, shows insincerity and sends messages out that they can't have anything important to say and are therefore not worthy of your attention. A big 'no no' in the building of life-confidence.

When your child is talking about something which is obviously important to them, respect this fact by giving them your fullest attention. Either stop what you are doing or, if it's an inconvenient time, explain this and arrange a time to listen when you are less preoccupied – and stick to it.

Look them in the eye; listen actively; listen attentively; listen reflectively. By this I mean get fully involved in what your child is saying; give them plenty of time to say what they want to say without interrupting or hurrying them; help them along if needs be with the odd question; then paraphrase and clarify what they have said to demonstrate to them that what they are saying is important to you and you have understood them.

 ROLE MODEL: Listening actively, with respect for what the other person has to say, is a key

ingredient in maintaining harmonious relationships and when you model this skill you will be demonstrating an important tool for your child to use when building their own relationships or resolving conflicts.

Listening With Empathy

In Stephen Covey's book *'The Seven Habits of Highly Effective People'* and his son Sean's book *'The Seven habits of Highly Effective Teenagers'* Habit #5 is 'Seek First to Understand, Then Be Understood'.

One of the strongest of human needs is the need to be understood and the ability to empathise is an invaluable life skill. Children go through immense frustration when they feel that adults don't understand them and recognising and understanding feelings is a powerful relationship skill.

One of the biggest problems teenagers have with their relationship with their parents is that they don't feel understood. Giving time to truly listen to understand – using your imagination and putting yourself in their skin – is crucial to keeping the channels of communication open.

With younger children, what may seem trivial to you, can be a big problem to them, and what they have to say needs to be respected. Children whose feelings are clearly not understood, for want of better listening skills of the adult, can feel most frustrated and this will have an effect on their confidence.

Take the times when your child falls and grazes her knees or hands. On more than one occasion during my teaching career, and also with my own children, when they fell and hurt themselves I have been guilty of saying, "Oh, that's nothing, only a little graze, don't cry", but – surprise, surprise – they usually continued to cry!

Can you remember the last time you fell and grazed yourself? Probably not! Well let me remind you. It HURTS!

I know – because it happened to me recently! I fell down in my garden and grazed my hands – 'Ouch!' Although there wasn't much to show for my pain, it really brought home to me how much it stings!

Let me tell you about Esme:

Esme's Story

A few days after my own fall, I was in school and a little girl called Esme was sent in at break time because she had fallen down. She was sobbing uncontrollably and no one had been able to console her.

She was still sobbing when I sat down with her. I looked at her hands and said, *"Ooooh, you poor soul, that really stings doesn't it? I know just how that feels!"*

You will not believe the effect those few words of understanding had! They worked like magic!

Esme instantly stopped crying and, what I can only describe as 'an air of relief' spread over her face. She relaxed completely!

I couldn't have taken the sting out more effectively if I had smothered her hands with ointment and given her pain killers!

There are two reasons why this approach worked so well. Firstly I helped her put into words how it feels when you graze your hand, (it stings) and secondly I took the trouble to let her know that I understood how she must be feeling, instead of dismissing her tears and sobs out of hand and telling her not to cry.

ROLE MODEL: Empathising is an important interpersonal skill for children to learn and it's important for us to lead by example. Empathising with a child's feelings is the first step towards teaching her to be empathetic with the feelings of others.

Avoiding Conflict

If there is one important thing to take away from this book it is this: Conflict between you and your child should be avoided whenever possible.

The parent/child relationship is an emotional one and because of this it can easily become volatile. Don't let it. It should be one of mutual respect whilst at the same time keeping the parent's position of authority intact.

As their children grow older, some parents fall into the trap of assuming the role of a best buddy and, in an effort to win the approval of their children, they let go of their authority role. This is a BIG mistake and places too much responsibility onto the shoulders of their children.

They definitely DON'T need a parent as a best friend – they will soon have plenty of friends in their lives if they haven't got them already and there will be plenty of time to be best friends with them when they are adults.

As well as unconditional love, respect and understanding, what children need most in this business of 'growing up', is security and guidance.

Guidance in the form of the backing and support of someone in authority who is more experienced than them and security meaning having definite boundaries in place defining what is acceptable and what is unacceptable behaviour – the reason for these boundaries being explained to them whenever possible.

So what do I mean by authority? The word 'authority' is synonymous with power and control. The Shorter Oxford Dictionary defines authority as, "Power or right to enforce obedience... those in power or control " However whilst a parent should have power and control, it is the interpretation of that power and the way control is exerted which is crucial to successful parenting.

There is the 'Because I said so!' power and control and then there is the quietly but firmly assertive power and control which explains 'the reason behind the rule'. The latter will, without question, earn the highest respect.

The 'Because I said so' approach may get an obedient response initially, but when applied too often, it will set you up for a defiant, argumentative child in the future, and is most certainly not a good role model for children to copy in their relationships with others.

A general theme which keeps cropping up as I write this book, is that an excess of negative commands brings the danger of them becoming ineffective (see Chapter 9 on saying 'No' and Chapter 16 on threats). So it is with rules – having too many of them will ultimately diminish their effectiveness. Keeping rules to the important things and always explaining the reason behind them is a good philosophy.

Once you have a rule in place and your child understands the reason for that rule, make sure you stick to it. Children are experts at manipulation and one of their methods is to draw you into lengthy arguments. Don't allow that to happen. Being quietly assertive is always more effective than ranting and raving.

This applies to all ages including teenagers. At all costs absolutely refuse to be drawn into arguments. They will get you nowhere and, where teenagers are concerned, they will only serve to break down lines of communication and once communication is cut off, you are lost.

Example 1 getting drawn in to an argument

Parent: *"Have a good time at the party. Don't forget, make sure you get home by 11 o'clock"*

Teenager: *"That's so unfair. Rob's mum lets him stay out until midnight"*

Parent: *"Well that's probably only on exceptional occasions"*

Teenager: *"No it's not – it's any time. He comes home even later at weekends"*

Parent: *"I'm sure that's not true, and anyway he's older than you"*

Teenager: *"Not that much older, anyway Will's my age and he's allowed to be in at 11.30"*

Parent: *"I'm sure that's not true"*

Teenager: *"It is true – ring his mum and ask her"*

Parent: *"I'm not ringing her now. I'll talk to her on Monday"*

Teenager: *"Why not now?"*

Parent: *"Because I'm about to cook dinner"*

Teenager: *"A phone call won't take long"*

Parent: (raising voice)

"Yes it will and I've got to be out by eight"

Teenager: *"Will's mum wouldn't be so strict"*

Parent (exasperated)

"Well I'm not Will's mum! I'm your mum!

Teenager: *"I wish you were Will's mum! Why can't I get in at 11.30?"*

Parent: (worn down)

"OK 11.30 then, just this once. But you'd better be in on time or you're grounded!"

The above dialogue is a classic example of the parent allowing themselves to be drawn in to an argument which ends in the parent being manipulated into giving in. It makes you feel exhausted just reading it!

Now look at this next example:

Example 2 being calmly assertive

Parent: *"Have a good time at the party. Don't forget, make sure you get home by 11 o'clock"*

Teenager: *"That's so unfair. Rob's mum lets him stay out until midnight"*

Parent: *"11 o'clock is our rule"*

Teenager: *"And he comes home even later at weekends"*

Parent: *"11 o'clock is our rule"*

Teenager: *"Will's my age and he's allowed to be in at 11.30"*

Parent: *"11 o'clock is our rule"*

Teenager: *"It's so unfair"*

Parent: (quietly) *"We'll review it on your birthday but for now, 11 o'clock is our rule. End of story"*

Here the parent is assertive without raising her voice. She also puts in a diffuser at the end *("We'll review it on your birthday")* to meet the teenager half way and bring the conversation to a halt.

The parent refuses to be swayed and makes it quite clear that the house rule is not open for negotiation at this moment in time. She needs to keep her promise to review it however, otherwise she won't be believed in future. When they review the curfew time, after allowing time for a civilised discussion and input from the child, she may extend it to show she is reasonable but she will then stick to that agreed time and maybe set a future date for reviewing. Children need the security of boundaries within the context of mutual respect and love.

To summarise: Self-love is a powerful ingredient of life-confidence and you can help your child to love himself in many ways.

- Respect his feelings
- Teach him to care about the feelings of others
- Be a good listener
- Help him understand and manage his emotions
- Build his self-worth, self-esteem and self-image
- Help him face his fears
- Avoid conflict

- Give him boundaries

- Be a good role model

- Love him unconditionally

And now for the final piece of The B.E.S.T. Success Formula. . .

The ACTION!

PART 5

The Fourth Pillar of

Life-Confidence:

Targeted
Action Steps

"Whatever you think you can do or believe you can do, begin it.
Action has magic, grace, and power in it"

Goethe

What Does it Mean?

Up until now we have dealt with what goes on on the *inside*. Now it's time to talk about putting that inner strength into outer action and transforming that positive mental attitude into tangible physical results.

To help you to really understand what I mean by Targeted Action Steps I'm going to take a minute to break this one up for you.

Targeted

Take Aim

This means targeted towards your main goal; it means keeping focused on what it is you want to ultimately achieve and, when other distractions get in the way, bringing yourself back on course.

Action

Walk The Thought

You've thought through your main dream goal. You've built your feelings of desire and enthusiasm. Action is the 'doing' part of the thinking and feeling. It's what I call 'walking the thought'

Steps

"How do you eat an elephant? One bite at a time"

Achieving a big dream goal is like eating that elephant – looking at it as a whole would be totally overpowering. Conquering a big challenge is a bit like climbing a mountain. If you were told to take one massive leap to the top you would say, *"Impossible"* and of course you'd be right. In fact, if you were focussing solely on the enormity of the task as a whole you would probably never even take that first step. You would be frozen with fear and would give up before you'd even started.

Focussing on that first small step however would be a different picture.

This would make the task much more manageable, and would free you up sufficiently to take action, and the ensuing success would give you confidence to take the next step and the next and so on to move you towards your goal.

Small changes are so much easier to tackle and many baby steps added together will eventually get you to the top of your 'mountain', whatever that mountain happens to be.

It's the same with any task which you find daunting. The secret to building that confidence and getting you moving forward is to break the task into small chunks or baby steps, which should stretch you a little outside your comfort zone, but which you feel capable of achieving.

Chapter 17

Get Out of That Comfort Zone

Here's the trick

Because you are human you will feel most comfortable when you are in a familiar routine, interacting with familiar people, in familiar surroundings with no demands being made of you. This is known as your 'comfort zone'

Unfortunately however, if we stay in our 'comfort zone' we very soon begin to feel lethargic, depressed and unfulfilled. In fact we are not truly living, we are merely existing.

A certain amount of nervousness is definitely good for us! (see Chapter 14 on Managing Your Feelings). Like it or not, it's a fact of life that if you want to grow and live a fulfilled life you will have to deal with the unfamiliar, take risks and move into unknown territory, and this brings with it some degree of fear.

Most actors will tell you that they need to feel slightly nervous in order to sharpen their mind and perform at their best. Life is like that. Stress hormones are produced to help us perform at our best.

The problem is, if we are too stressed and fearful then we are incapable of thinking clearly and, at worse, we become totally immobilised by our fear. That's when we move into our 'terror zone'.

The trick is to make sure we are stretching ourselves just enough to be growing and moving forward – in other words in our 'stretch zone' – but not enough to take us into our 'terror zone'.

And the rewards far outweigh the initial discomfort.

An example of this might be someone who is afraid of speaking in public. Put this person in front of an audience and they would quite likely have a mental block. However if they were first to succeed with giving their speech to one other person, then to two people, then a small group, they would gradually gain sufficient confidence at each step to move on to the next one until they were finally ready to speak in front of a larger gathering (it's eating that elephant again).

What happens is this: Each time we stretch ourselves our comfort zone expands and our self-confidence expands with it, and what once seemed scary eventually becomes second nature to us.

And that's how we grow. . .

So this. . .

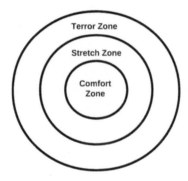

Becomes this. . .

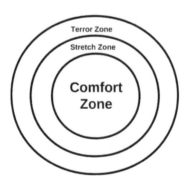

For children, their 'elephant' or 'mountain' might be something like putting their hand up in class discussion, or perhaps diving off a high diving board at the swimming pool. The same 'Baby Step Rule' applies: for example, practising contributing when in a small group until sufficient confidence is gained to take part in a larger one; practising jumping from the side of the pool, then from the low board and so on until confident to go higher.

A good example of baby steps demonstrated by schools is the myriad of tests which children are now given, ranging from spellings and tables tests to mock SATs papers, all to prepare them for the real thing. As a result they have much more confidence, when taking their SATs, than they would otherwise have had (the one good thing which comes out of children being given test papers until they are coming out of their ears!).

To help your child to expand their comfort zone try to encourage them to operate in their stretch zone when you can.

Talk to your child about situations which they are comfortable about; ones which are a little uncomfortable and ones which are plain scary. Just like everyone has a different pain threshold, so we each have a different stretch zone threshold according to what we are doing.

When I am teaching I am constantly checking that the children are being stretched just enough. We have a 'Zone Communication Code' whereby at the end of a piece of work they draw a smiley face if they found it easy, a face with a straight mouth if they found it stretched them a bit and a sad face if it was really hard.

This is particularly useful to me when marking homework when I haven't got the children with me.

For class activities which are not recorded I ask for a 'thumbs up' if they found it easy, 'thumbs horizontal' if they were stretched and 'thumbs down' if it was too difficult.

You can get your children to let you know which zone they are in, in various situations.

Examples:

Riding a horse

Petting a friend's dog

Playing a piece of music

Doing homework

Doing a Test

Swimming

Gym

Taking part in the school play

In this way you can make sure they are always being stretched just enough to grow.

A Word About 'Failure'

To achieve anything worth achieving in life we must be prepared for setbacks. Even if you 'screw your courage to the sticking post' there will be times when you fail to achieve the desired results.

The fact is:

 Failing is a necessary part of success.

Edison 'failed' over a thousand times when working on a project but when it was suggested that it must be discouraging he said that he had merely learnt 1,000 ways that 'the thing couldn't be done'! Here is an excerpt of what he is purported to have said:

"After we had conducted thousands of experiments on a certain project without solving the problem, one of my associates, after we had conducted the crowning experiment and it had proved a failure, expressed discouragement and disgust over our having failed to find out anything. I cheerily assured him that we had learned something. For we had learned for a certainty that the

thing couldn't be done that way, and that we would have to try some other way."[6]

Now that's the way to deal with failure.

The point is this: Only when you are constantly emotionally involved with your goals will you be armed to withstand the inevitable setbacks. Only then will you regard failures as valuable lessons and only then will you be moved into the action needed to overcome them.

As Paul Hudsey put it: *"The only way to overcome the fear of failure, is to have a goal worth failing for"* And to have a goal that's exciting enough to make it worth failing for, it needs to be a goal of your own making. It may take some tweaking and re-thinking, but once you have finally found something that 'lights your fire', stick with it.

Set a date for your main goal but don't be disheartened if you have underestimated how long it will take you to achieve it. As long as you are working towards it there is no shame in changing the date – but keep the goal. Be persistent.

In Sir Winston Churchill's famous words, *"Never give up!"*

 Mistakes can be used to our advantage as they are opportunities to learn and grow. However, there is a huge difference between saying, "I'm a failure" and "I have failed" – the first focuses on the person and stifles desire, the second focuses on the task and allows room for rising to the challenge and focussing on the solution to the problem. The distinction between these two concepts must be borne in mind when helping your children to overcome setbacks without denting their confidence.

---

[6]from an interview with Edison (American Magazine Jan 1921).

Chapter 18

Goal Achieving

Walking the Thought
Mental Rehearsal

So continuous small successes then are crucial. This is what keeps you from giving up on your dream. To satisfy the need to feel you are progressing, make sure you break your goal down into those manageable, achievable 'baby steps' or 'journey goals' which are not too daunting. And be sure to check in regularly to make sure your journey goals are congruent with your main goal. All this of course applies to your child as well.

Some adults say they had known what they wanted to be for as long as they could remember, e.g. they had a vocation for nursing or for teaching. However the majority of children don't know what they want and even if they do know, they are likely to change their minds as they mature and gain experience.

If your child is unsure about what he would like to achieve, perhaps he could think of a person he admires, someone he would like to emulate. Maybe his dream is to be a great football player or to work with animals. No matter what it is, as long as he has a dream to focus on and it's something he truly want, that's fine. It's that dream which will give him the motivation to be the best he can be.

Let's say he is telling you about all the exciting things he wants to be, do and have and being the good listener you have learnt to be – you are giving him the space to use his imagination and become emotionally involved. You must be totally non-judgemental and encourage him in his aspirations. Whether he says he wants to be a rocket scientist or a road sweeper, a brain surgeon or a barman, you receive the information with equal non judgement. As long as it is something which is humanly possible to do, you must encourage him to believe he can do it. The only proviso being that it doesn't impinge on the rights of others. Apart from that, the sky's the limit.

⚠ **Remember what we have said about limiting beliefs in Part 2. It's important here not to allow your own limiting beliefs to cause you to react incredulously if your child says something which you think is unlikely to happen.**

Next, ask your child to go forward in time and imagine he has become the person he wants to be (visualisation). How does he feel? What is he doing? What are people saying? The idea with children is to get them excited about their dreams.

As Stephen Covey puts it, *"Begin with the end in mind"*

Now – once you have nurtured a big dream, you can then come back to the present. And here's the link:

To achieve most things in life we need to have the basics of literacy and numeracy and a basic knowledge of other subjects covered in school. This links what your child needs to do now (try hard with his school work) with his highest value (achieving his dream).

Talk this one through with your child and see how many ways you can come up with, whereby doing well at school will be of benefit to him in achieving his goal. For example we need to earn money to buy the things we want, either in a job or as a self-employed person.

Now we can look at the first baby step:

Having established that school is important you can then explore what area he would like to improve first which will move him towards his goal.

Children respond brilliantly to incisive questions like, "If you could wave a magic wand what would you like to improve?" or "What would you do if you knew you couldn't fail?"

Get him to brainstorm what he could do to achieve what he'd like to achieve. Success with the baby steps will go a long way towards boosting his confidence.

These baby steps should be S.M.A.R.T. steps:

Specific, **M**easurable, **A**chievable, **R**ealistic and **T**ime phased.

Here's an example of a S.M.A.R.T. baby step:

Child: *"If I could wave a magic wand I would get 10/10 for my tables test"*

Adult: *"By when?"*

Child: *"By next week"*

Adult: *"OK. Which tables do you need to practise?"*

Child: *"My threes"*

Adult: *"Hmmm. Let's look at the ones you know already"*

Child: *"I know 2x3 that's pip squeak"*

Adult: *"What else?"*

Child: *"Well I know 3x3, 4x3 and 5x3"*

Adult: *"That's good! What else?"*

Child: *"Well I know 10x3 'cos you just add a nought, and for 11x3 you just put two threes"*

Adult: *"What else?"*

Child: *"I don't know the others, they're hard to learn"*

Adult: *"Well, let's see. You know 2x3, 3x3, 4x3, 5x3, 10x3 and 11x3 so you've got 6x3, 7x3, 8x3, 9x3 and 12x3 to learn. So you've just got 5 to learn and 5 days before your test"*

Child: *"I could learn one every day"*

Adult: *"Great! Which one shall we start with?"*

You now have a Specific goal which your child has set; it's Measurable; you have broken it down into Achievable baby steps; it's Realistic; you have a Time frame. It may only be a baby step towards improving, but it's a baby step in the right direction and when you allow the time and space for your child to work out their own actions, they are far more likely to carry them out.

Some children may not know what they want to do long-term, an exciting goal for them might be to make more friends, be in the school play or join the school football team – that's great. If your child comes up with shorter term goals, you simply apply the same approach: help them to break their goal into manageable baby steps whilst keeping the end in mind.

The emphasis in the goal setting process must be placed on the fact that children need to have ownership of their goals. It must come from them. It must be in line with their own set of values – not yours.

ROLE MODEL: Make sure your child is aware of you setting your own goals. Let him see you planning your week. Set aside some time, say each weekend, when you sit down together and plan your weekly baby steps individually. You might want to have a set template to fill in to make it more special and easier to follow.

Walking the Thought

A very clever way to programme the mind is to play the acting game. Actually act as if you are already that person in possession of your desires.

How would that person feel? How would they walk, talk, sit, dress? If your goal is to be more assertive act as if you are already assertive; if you want to be attractive act as if you are attractive and so on. This also works well with self-confidence. Regularly practise acting as if you are already the confident person you want to be until your whole body language shouts "I'm a winner".

When faced with a situation which you are a little unsure of, think about how that 'confident you' would behave, what they would say, how they would feel and what their posture would be like. (Your sub-conscious mind knows all the answers) Then go right ahead and act out the part. Children can be helped greatly by this approach.

It's a fact that if we act out the part for long enough on a regular basis, the sub-conscious mind will take it on board and we will actually start to turn into the person we want to be.

Famous film star and heart throb of the 50's, Gregory Peck, once said,

"I acted like Gregory Peck for so long, I became him!"

Children are of course, often better at these games than we are. They don't have such a large accumulation of limiting thoughts as we have.

Use the 'Act As If' approach as often as possible with your child.

 ACTION: Leverage your child's imagination with the 'Act As If' game. Talk her through the sort of person she wants to be. Get her to describe herself in detail using all her senses. Get her to draw a picture of her new self and write about it; even give it a name. The object is to get her as emotionally involved in it as possible. Once she has established an image of that cool, self-confident person you can remind her of that when she is faced with a challenge. Ask "Well what would x do?" or "How would x react?" Do this often enough and she will start to become that person!

Mental Rehearsal

Another exercise advocated by Maxwell Maltz (see also Chapters 4 and 12) is the Mental Rehearsal exercise.

The way it works is this: If you have a particularly challenging situation coming up, take time to quietly go within and mentally rehearse exactly how you want it to be. Imagine yourself feeling confident and in control of the situation. Imagine what you are saying and what your posture is like and imagine the positive response of the people around you. Fill in as much detail as possible. Do this with your child as often as necessary to build his confidence.

Here are some examples:

Starting a new school

Going into hospital

Making new friends

Going for an interview

Taking a test

Coping with assertive peers

Talking to the teacher

The list is endless and the more your child enters into this pretend game the quicker it will start to become his reality.

One client of mine came to me with a problem of chronic lack of confidence and low self-esteem. She was due to go for an interview for medical school but was so shy that she was unable to have a conversation with anyone other than her family and one or two close friends.

When in unfamiliar situations, she was so fearful of what others might think of her that her body would be seized with tension and she would begin to shake.

I took this client through a series of Guided Visualisations. A Guided Visualisation is a situation which you conjure up in your imagination whilst someone talks you through it or 'tells the story'(see Chapter 12)

Firstly she visualised herself talking confidently to people she didn't know. She put this into practice setting herself mini goals like saying hello to one new person each day, then slowly increasing the length of conversations.

After getting her to describe exactly how she would like her interview to be she subsequently imagined herself walking into the interview room brimming with confidence and self-assurance.

The outcome was a hugely successful interview and a totally transformed young lady who was absolutely 'over the moon'!

At the time of writing this I have just received an ecstatic email from this client saying she has been accepted! However the point in question is this – she felt a huge success even before the interview, and even if she hadn't received an offer she would have been able to accept the outcome without letting it dent her confidence.

Now here's the exciting bit!!

 Guided Visualisation is particularly effective when used with children by the very nature of the fact that they are very receptive to the power of suggestion and have such great, wild, vivid imaginations!

Here's an example:

Suppose your child was about to start her first day at her new school and she was worried about not making friends. Get her to tell you how she would like it to be. Ask her to close her eyes and imagine all the details – running a mental movie on the screen of her mind.

Ask her to tell you what's happening i.e. *"So you are arriving at school, who do you meet first?" "What are they saying?" "How are you feeling?" "What happens next?" "Who else do you meet?"* Only positive images are allowed.

In my opinion this is a tool much under utilised in schools, but the great thing is, parents can do much to redress the balance.

It's a fact that whilst outside circumstances and the things other people say and do are often outside our control, the one thing we can control is the way we react to them and when children are empowered to take control of how they deal with life their life-confidence will rocket sky-high!

PART 6

Over to You!

"Take responsibility for yourself
because no one's going to take responsibility for you"
Tyra Banks

Chapter 19

The Way Forward

Start Now!
A Brief Summary of The B.E.S.T. Success Formula
Using The B.E.S.T. Success Formula
Where Do You Go From Here? – Suggested Actions
The 3 R's
Have No Regrets
A Final Word
Reading and Listening

Start Now!

So are you ready for action?

It cannot be overemphasised that all the reading in the world will not bring results unless you put in the necessary ACTION!

This is a statement of the obvious, but one that we need to remind ourselves of, time and time again. It's crucial that you begin straight away to integrate the ideas from this book into your everyday life, whilst they are still fresh in your mind. Begin at once to try them out until they become a way of life for both you and your children.

Children are very adaptable and forgiving. As you work through the stages be honest with them and apologise if you make mistakes. Being able to say sorry is a good lesson for them to learn. The main thing is to get started, and above all ... START NOW!

A Brief Summary of the B.E.S.T. Success Formula

To summarise The B.E.S.T. Success Formula –

- It's simple yet profound.

- It covers the four most important areas of development each of which is indispensable for building life-confidence.

- It's a fail-safe set of strategies which are guaranteed to improve the quality of life for anyone who is prepared to apply them diligently.

- It is based on the premise that both you and your child are capable of achieving great things.

To help you get started, here's an outline of the main ingredients of The B.E.S.T. Success Formula which you will need to apply consistently on a regular daily basis:

1. BELIEF – BELIEVE IN YOURSELF – BELIEVE IN YOUR CHILD – HELP THEM BUILD THEIR OWN SELF-BELIEF – YOU CAN DO IT

- Reinforce your own self-belief every day by reminding yourself of that awesome potential you have hidden within your mind.

- Inspire your child with the knowledge that he is capable of achieving great things by letting him see you truly believe in him.

- Remember to apply the three stages of consciousness to every area you wish to change.

2. ENTHUSIASM – BUILD YOUR GOALS AROUND YOUR PASSIONS – BUILD THE DREAM

- Get enthusiastic together.

- Be true to your values.

- Acknowledge the fact that your child's values may be different from your own.

- Develop your imagination and that of your child in order to create that strong desire needed to move you into action.

3. SELF-LOVE – FOSTER A STRONG SELF-ESTEEM AND SELF-WORTH – MAKE YOURSELF FEEL WORTHY TO RECEIVE

- Turn yourself into someone worthy of being loved.

- Help your child to do the same.

- Be yourself. You are at your most powerful when you are being your authentic self.

- Let your child know that you accept him just the way he is. Make your love totally unconditional.

- Bring balance and serenity into your life by neutralising your emotions and seeing the challenges and drawbacks in everything.

- Make your child aware of challenges and drawbacks too.

4. TARGETED ACTION STEPS – TAKE BABY STEPS TOWARDS YOUR GOAL – ACT AS IF

- Tap into your inner strength.

- Plan those baby steps which will move you towards your main goal.

- Walk the thought and act like you've arrived.

- Help your child to do the same. Bring out the actor in him and build on those small successes to build belief.

USING THE B.E.S.T. SUCCESS FORMULA

The following are some examples of how The B.E.S.T. Success Formula can be applied to specific situations:

Making new friends

1. Belief

- Believe you can make friends.
- Call on past strengths – When have you made friends in the past?
- What did you do then? How did it make you feel?
- Write affirmations.

e.g. *"I am a great friend" "I am very popular" "Everyone wants to be my friend" "I am caring" "I am fun to be with"*

2. Enthusiasm

- Build the picture of how you would like things to be. What kind of friend would you like to have? What qualities would they have? (kind, thoughtful, fun, etc).
- Visualise yourself going up to this person and opening up the conversation.
- Imagine how you are feeling.
- Imagine how they are looking – smiling, laughing at your jokes, chatting.

3. Self-love

- What ways can you make yourself into a person someone would want as a friend? (smile, offer to help, share your things, be good fun, show you care etc – be all the things that you want your friend to be).
- Make yourself feel worthy by thinking of all the good things about yourself.
- Get rid of feelings of neediness. Be your own best friend.

4. Targeted Action Steps

- Set yourself a target to speak to someone new each day.
- What will you do to practise 'Acting As If' you are confident? (smile, make eye contact, walk tall etc).

Going for an interview

1. Belief

- Believe in your ability.
- Programme your mind with only positive thoughts about the outcome.
- Use affirmations.

  e.g. *"I am more than capable of doing this job" "They are very lucky to have the chance of employing me" "I am clear thinking and I express myself well" "Whatever the outcome I can handle it" "I am coping well"* etc.

- Call on past times when you have been nervous but you have still achieved good results.
- Think of all the people who have faith in you.

2. Enthusiasm

- Take time to run your mental movie of you relaxing and enjoying the interview.
- See yourself smiling and in control.
- Visualise yourself shaking hands confidently and being congratulated.
- 'Act As If' you are full of confidence.

3. Self-love

- Remind yourself that you are special.
- Know that you have done your best to prepare for the interview and that the outcome will depend on many factors which are out of your control.
- Know that it is an opportunity to grow.

4. Targeted Action Steps

- Write out a preparation plan.

- Break it into a programme of baby steps and fit it into the time available.

- Arrange mock interviews (Act As If).

- Speak to other people with relevant knowledge.

- Research the company.

Where Do You Go From Here? – Suggested Actions

So! We are nearly at the end of this book – but this is only the beginning!

I have taken so much pleasure in writing this for you but the biggest reward for me is if you make yourself a promise to start using everything you have learnt to build your child's confidence. Here are some suggestions as to what you could do next:

• Re-Read This Book

Then revisit those three areas you chose at the beginning and take a moment now to jot down, highlight or bookmark any ideas or insights you have gained from this book which you could take away with you and apply to those areas.

• Write Down Your Action Plan

Next, take each area individually, decide on the approach you are going to use to improve, and write down an action plan as a reminder.

• Keep a Success Diary

Try keeping a diary of your successes and reflect upon how effective your strategies were. What worked today? What didn't work? What needs to be tried out again another time?

• Talk to Others

Who needs to know about your new strategies? Take time to talk to other adults involved in caring for your children, and explain why you would like to try a certain approach.

• Talk to Your Children

Take time to talk to your children. If they are old enough to under-stand, tell them that there are going to be some changes.

Tell them why – explain that you have sometimes made mistakes and you want to make sure you are being really fair with them. They will respect you for it and will be far more likely to co-operate.

• Join forces

Join forces with other positive-thinking, like-minded parents for mutual support. Share this book. Meet up regularly to compare notes and share your successes.

• Read other books

You can't have too much of a good thing! Try dipping into the recommended reading below.

• Get one-to-one help and support

If you would like to find out how life-confidence coaching can help you or your child you can get in touch by emailing me at:

sue@lifeconfidenceforkids.com

For more information and to receive your free eBook go to

www.lifeconfidenceforkids.com

or visit our Facebook Fan Page: "Life Confidence For Kids".

I look forward to helping you on your life-confidence journey.

I'm going to leave you with a quick reference check list of the most important things to remember about your relationship with your children:

The 3 R's

(Apologies for the title – it's the teacher in me!)
Respect – Recognition – Reassurance

Respect

- Respect your child's feelings
- Respect their dreams and desires
- Respect the fact that they need to be understood
- Respect the fact that they need to be listened to
- Respect the things which are important to them
- Respect their need to be taken seriously
- Respect their presence

Recognition

- Recognise your child's need for the space to grow
- Recognise their need to make their own mistakes
- Recognise the need to give them responsibilities
- Recognise their strengths
- Recognise their huge potential
- Recognise their need to be appreciated simply for who they are
- Recognise they need to be allowed to take certain risks
- Recognise the need to spend quality time
- Recognise the value in accentuating the positive
- Recognise the need to help them express their feelings in words
- Recognise the need to help them become independent
- Recognise the need for them to learn to respect others
- Recognise the need for them to learn to respect themselves

Reassurance

- Reassure them that you are always there for them
- Reassure them of your belief in them
- Reassure them they are special and worthy
- Reassure them of your everlasting unconditional love

Have No Regrets

Children grow up oh so quickly! However many times you hear that cliché, it's a fact that you only realise the truth of it when they have grown up!

I was sorting through my photograph box the other day, pondering, as you do, over nostalgic memories.

As I looked at photos of my children when they were young, it made me realise how fleeting those years had been. I saw those innocent little people with new eyes after all these years.

I realised that, when I was caught up in the treadmill of life as a mum – all the washing, the cleaning, the tidying, the school run, the homework, the taxiing to and from clubs and sleepovers – I hadn't taken enough time to stand and stare at my children and count my blessings.

Too often we are so caught up in the rush and hurry of life that we don't appreciate our children as much as we really should.

Make that time to spend with them – have no regrets.

A Final Word

Someone once said that each time you read a good book over again, you don't find anything in it that wasn't there before, you find something in *you* that you didn't see before.

I would like to thank you for reading this one and it is my hope that you will read it over again many times and discover something new about yourself and your children each time you do.

I have no doubt that Social and Emotional Intelligence will eventually play a key role in every school.

Until then, by studying the concepts set out here and putting them into practice, you will be equipped with the knowledge and understanding of an area of education which will be instrumental in helping your children, and your children's children, to live long, happy and fulfilled lives. In short, you will equip them with the one true secret of life-success – **Supreme Life-Confidence!**

Reading and Listening

There are many self-development and parenting books on the market to choose from. Here are some I can personally recommend (in no particular order):

PARENTING
What Do You Really Want For Your Children? (CD set) – Dr Wayne Dyer
How to Talk So Kids Will Listen and Listen So Kids Will Talk – Adele Faber and Elaine Mazlish
How to Talk So Teens Will Listen and Listen So Teens Will Talk – Adele Faber and Elaine Mazlish
The Secret of Happy Children – Steve Biddulph
Screamer to Sweet Dreamer – Lorraine Thomas
Raising Happy Kids for Dummies – Sue Atkins
Raising Teenagers – Lynn Huggins-Cooper
Confident Teens – Gael Lindenfield
Dr D's Lifeskills Toolkit 4 Kids and Teens – Dr John F Demartini
The 7 Habits of Highly Effective Teenagers – Sean Covey
Relax Kids – The Wishing Star – Marneta Viegas
Relax Kids – Aladdin's Magic Carpet – Marneta Viegas

PERSONAL DEVELOPMENT
Feel the Fear and Do It Anyway – Susan Jeffers
End the Struggle and Dance With Life – Susan Jeffers
Psycho-Cybernetics – Maxwell Maltz
The 7 Habits of Highly Effective People – Stephen Covey
The Breakthrough Experience – Dr John F Demartini
Instant Confidence (Book and CD) – Paul McKenna
What to Say When You Talk to Yourself – Shad Helmstetter
Your Winner's Image (DVD/CD set) – Bob Proctor
You Were Born Rich – Bob Proctor

Lightning Source UK Ltd.
Milton Keynes UK
UKHW011044070819
347551UK00003B/643/P